FROM THE PROTOCOLS OF THE ELDERS OF ZION TO HOLOCAUST DENIAL TRIALS

This volume is dedicated to three men who have made Jewish Studies and the Conference from which this volume emerged possible: Richard Freeland, former President of Northeastern University, Boston, who encouraged and supported the conference, James Stellar, Dean of the College of Arts and Sciences, who made Jewish Studies possible at Northeastern University, and Bill Giessen, Professor of Chemistry and Associate Director of the Barnett Institute, who had the vision for Jewish Studies long before it was a reality.

All proceeds for the book will be given to the Jewish Studies Program at Northeastern University.

From the Protocols of the Elders of Zion to Holocaust Denial Trials

Challenging the Media, the Law and the Academy

Editors

Debra Kaufman
Gerald Herman
James Ross
David Phillips

with the help of Jennifer Fagen

Foreword by
Deborah Lipstadt

VALLENTINE MITCHELL
LONDON • PORTLAND, OR

First published in 2007 in Great Britain by
VALLENTINE MITCHELL
Suite 314, Premier House, 112–114 Station Road, Edgware, Middlesex HA8 7BJ

and in the United States of America by
VALLENTINE MITCHELL
c/o ISBS, 920 NE 58th Avenue, Suite 300, Portland, OR 97213 3786
Portland, Oregon, 97213-3786

Website: www.vmbooks.com

Copyright collection 2007 Vallentine Mitchell
Individual chapters © Individual authors

British Library Cataloguing in Publication Data:

A catalogue record for this book has been applied for

ISBN 978 0 85303 641 8 (cloth)
ISBN 978 0 85303 642 5 (paper)

Library of Congress Cataloging-in-Publication Data:

A catalog record for this book has been applied for

All rights reserved. No part of this publication may be reproduced, stored in or introduced into a retrieval system, or transmitted, in any form or by any means, electronic, mechanical, photocopying, recording or otherwise without the prior written permission of the publisher of this book.

Printed in Great Britain by Biddles Ltd, King's Lynn, Norfolk

Contents

	Dedication	ii
	Foreword by Deborah Lipstadt	vii
1	Introduction *Debra Kaufman, Gerald Herman, David Phillips and James Ross*	1
2	Libeling the Jews: Truth Claims, Trials, and the Protocols of Zion *Stephen Eric Bronner*	15
3.	The Media and the Holocaust: Protocols of the Elders of Zion – Then and Now *Robert L. Hilliard*	25
4.	The Protocols of the Elders of Zion: Group Defamation Trials in Civil Courts and the 'Court' of Public Opinion *Frederick M. Lawrence*	37
5.	The Persistence of Falsehood and the Protocols of the Elders of Zion *Martha Minow*	47
6.	The Holocaust and its (Re)Telling: The Nature of Evidence at the Nuremberg and Eichmann Trials *Tim Cole*	56

7. The Surprising Historic Roots
   of Holocaust Denial
   Henry L. Feingold — 67

8. Jewish Victims in a Wartime Frame:
   A Press Portrait of the Nuremberg Trial
   Laurel Leff — 80

9. Jewish Identity, the International Tribunal
   at Nuremberg and the Eichmann Trial
   Allan A. Ryan — 102

10. Dirty Work: A Personal Reflection on
    the Irving Trial
    Robert Jan van Pelt — 111

    List of Editors and Contributors — 121

    Index — 125

Foreword

When I learned that David Irving was threatening a libel suit against me because I described him in my book *Denying the Holocaust: The Growing Assault on Truth and Memory* as a Holocaust denier who bends the truth until it fits his preconceived ideological notions, I laughed. Irving's unambiguous record of denial made this seem an idle threat. It soon became clear, however, that he was quite serious and that his action might actually lead to a court case. At that point my main worry was how history would fare in the courtroom.

In the past I had been approached by people who wanted to bring legal action against Holocaust deniers, but I always cautioned them not to. The First Amendment practically guaranteed their failure. Even in countries where Holocaust denial could be outlawed, I opposed such efforts. These laws render denial 'forbidden fruit', making it more – not less – alluring. Above all, however, I did not believe that courtrooms are the proper venue for historical inquiry. Deniers, I argued, should be stopped with reasoned inquiry, not with the blunt edge of the law. Courts, it seemed to me, dispensed justice by having parties present what they consider compelling evidence, such as physical proof and hard facts, to convince a jury or judge according to a high standard of proof. Historians try to establish historical 'truth' by considering the context and circumstance of an event or a document. They interpret evidence and offer their most reasoned opinions aware that other historians may look at the same material and, without engaging in any deception, reach differing conclusions. Historians also know that as new sources and documents come to light, their 'truths' may be set aside. Simply put, historical truths cannot be measured like smog or toxins.

Then came my trial and its stunning victory. History and the forensic process seemed in perfect syncronization. In the aftermath, some people proclaimed that my solid victory proved that there was no conflict between these two systems. In fact, *Irving* v. *Penguin UK and Lipstadt* proved no such thing. The reason was quite simply expressed by my barrister, Richard Rampton, in his opening and closing statement, 'David Irving is a liar'. David Irving was not an iconoclastic historian with quirky or untenable views. The Holocaust was not on trial, I was. Therefore, our objective was to prove, not precisely what happened, but that I was correct when I said this man was a denier and a liar. We did so by putting his claims on trial. In short, we turned him into the defendant.

And we succeeded mightily, as is demonstrated by the judge's unequivocal declaration that Irving's conclusions were 'at odds with the documentary evidence', and that he 'serious[ly] misrepresent[ed] the available contemporaneous evidence', and posed arguments that were 'based upon misrepresentation, misconstruction, and omission of the documentary evidence'. He 'whitewash[ed]' evidence. The judge found Irving's claims about the authenticity of certain documents 'reprehensible' and he dismissed Irving's conclusions as 'absurd'.[1] The judgment was an unrelenting 300-page condemnation of Irving's assertions about the Holocaust, the bombing of Dresden and so much more.

For an encounter with an adversary such as Irving, the courtroom proved to be the perfect venue. Until this trial few, if any, historians had invested their time and energy to follow Irving's footnotes and document the discrepancies and falsifications in his work. They condemned his conclusions, but did not bother, for logical reasons, to waste their time tracking the bases of his absurd claims. Irving was left free to pose all sorts of arguments without anyone challenging him on the details. In the courtroom it was different. Irving could not simply float one of his 'theories'. There were experts, lawyers, and, most significantly, a judge present, all of whom could demand that he provide evidence to prove his claims. And, of course, he could not.

Shortly after our lead historical expert, Richard Evans, began to analyze Irving's work, he told me about some of his findings: 'Irving's veneer of respectability slips away as you do the research.' He admitted that he was surprised by the number of distortions he and his researchers had already found. 'There are simply too many for them to be mistakes. And they always seem to move in one direction: exoneration of Hitler.' In light of his comments, I suggested that, instead of arguing that David Irving is a sloppy or bad historian, Evans posited that he was no historian. Evans dismissed this out of hand. 'It is an absurd semantic dispute to declare someone who has written two dozen books about history not to be a historian at all. No judge or jury will accept it.' He said this with a finality that seemed to brook no debate.

About six months later, when Evans completed his report, he had dramatically changed his opinion:

> If we mean by historian someone who is concerned to discover the truth about the past and to give as accurate a representation of it as possible, then Irving is not a historian ... Irving is essentially an ideologue who uses history ... in order to further his own political purposes ...

Evans concluded that 'not one of [Irving's] books, speeches or articles, not one paragraph, not one sentence in any of them, can be taken on trust as an accurate representation of its historical subject. All of them are completely worthless as history...'[2] Evans's encounter with the evidence had convinced him that I was correct.

Repeatedly during the trial, particularly when David Irving vainly insisted that his point was valid even though all the evidence proved it was not, he appeared to me not just as a falsifier of history, but as an irrational, foolish and even pathetic figure. Since the trial, whenever his name appears in the press, it is almost invariably accompanied by some variation on the adjectival phrase: 'the Holocaust denier whom the court branded a racist, an antisemite, and a falsifier of history'.[3]

In Courtroom 73 in the Royal High Court in London, during the winter of 2000, history – not the Holocaust – was on trial. It passed the test, in part because of a wise judge, experts who did fastidious research and outstanding lawyers. It also passed the test because our task was to prove my opponent had no regard for history. We did not have to prove precisely what happened. The latter might be impossible to achieve in certain settings, as some of the contributors to this volume argue. The former was not.

NOTES

1. The Hon. Mr Charles Gray, 'Judgment', *Irving* v. *Penguin, UK and Deborah Lipstadt.* For full text see www.hdot.org, 'Judgment'.
2. Richard Evans, *David Irving, Hitler and Holocaust Denial, Expert Opinion, Irving* v. *Penguin and Deborah Lipstadt*, 1.6.1–1.6.2, 6.2.1, pp. 19–20, 739, available at www.hdot.org, 'Evidence'.
3. *Observer*, 3 March 2002. See also *Sunday Star-Times* (Auckland, New Zealand), 10 March 2002; *Evening Standard* (London), 28 March 2002, *Independent* (London), 23 April 2003, *The Age* (Australia), 7 May 2003.

1

Introduction

'From the *Protocols of the Elders of Zion* to the Deniers of the Holocaust: Challenging the Academy, the Press and the Legal System', was the title of the international conference held on 1–2 May 2001 at Northeastern University, Boston, MA and from which this volume of essays emerges. The immediate impetus for the conference was the impending trial involving David Irving and Deborah Lipstadt. David Irving sued American historian Deborah Lipstadt, author of *Denying the Holocaust* (1989), and her British publisher, Penguin Books, for labeling him a Holocaust denier. Irving's claim that the Nazis had no systematic program to murder all the Jews of Europe, and that camps run by the Germans were not meant to be extermination camps, depended on his insistence and 'proof' that Auschwitz, as the 'flagship' of all extermination camps, was not a gas chamber but rather a labor camp. Irving argued that the available evidence,[1] or the lack thereof, justified his conclusions. Those who had died there, he claimed, had died as victims of war and disease, and not of genocide. 'The trial,' writes D. D. Guttenplan, '… will almost inevitably be used by some to claim legitimacy for Holocaust "revisionism"'[2].

Each contributor to this book reflects on the ways in which evidence is presented, constructed and reconstructed from their disciplinary focus, and the ways in which historical truths are reconstructed and/or refuted over time. Not only was Lipstadt on trial, but history itself was on trial. The very methods whereby witness testimony, reportage and data are transformed through historical interpretation into knowledge, and knowledge into 'truth', were put on trial. This volume is concerned not only with contemporary Holocaust denial, but with the way in which key institutions such as the law, history and the media make truth claims, and what effect such investigations and exposés have on popular beliefs. Faced with proliferating printed and web-based assertions and reassertions of premises whose veracity have long since been disproved (such as those of the *Protocols of Zion*), we felt it important to provide our colleagues and students with a text that would step back from the Holocaust itself to the broader questions involved in the study of invective and hate. That is, how truth assertions are made and the ways in which they are maintained and/or dismantled over time. In this manner, we hope to achieve a deeper understanding about historical truths by confronting the methods by which the truth of assertions related to the fate of Jews in the twentieth century have been put forward, struggled over, and fixed in the law, in historical canon and in the popular imagination. We believe that the chapters in this book serve this larger purpose by focusing on those moments when historical facts are subjected to public test. By so doing, the essays provide salutary lessons to those who wish to understand the stubborn persistence of myths, even when confronted by the truth, and the power and limitations of the tools used by scholars, lawyers and journalists in their efforts to supplant those myths.

Robert Jan van Pelt, Professor of Architecture at the University of Waterloo, one of the contributors to this volume and an expert historian for the Irving/Lipstadt trial, begins his compelling book, *The Case for Auschwitz: Evidence from the Irving Trial* (2002) with a description of the media's response to Deborah Lipstadt's stunning victory over David Irving. Citing the *Irish Times*, van Pelt notes that the Lipstadt victory represented a 'calculated' and 'methodical destruction' of Irving's 'untruthful version of history'.[3] The *Guardian*, he writes, comments that 'there is now no room for doubt ... After this case, we can rely on empiricism and the sheer weight of evidence'[4] (emphasis ours). But can we rely on empiricism and the 'sheer weight of evidence'? Michael A. Hoffman II, a defender of Irving and a Holocaust denier, takes comfort (and in so doing foreshadows the fear of the editors and contributors to this volume about the seeming 'victory of history over hate') in the assertion that 'Great libel trials are dramas that stick in the memory for generations ... and posterity often takes a very different view than contemporary received opinion'.[5] Despite Lipstadt's momentous victory, we knew then, and know now, that 'final' verdicts cannot be taken for granted. Legal judgments do not necessarily determine either the quality or the prominence of the reporting of that outcome.

For instance, will the legal record, received historical wisdom and contemporary received opinion associated with the 'final' verdict of the *Irving* v. *Lipstadt* Trial, prove any more a deterrent to the resurgence of denial and anti-Semitism in the future than, for instance, earlier proceedings and historical renderings of the *Protocols of Zion*? How is it that nearly a hundred years after the *Protocols* first made their appearance, there are those who still believe that a small group of Jews manipulate and control the world, as recent reports from right-wing websites in the United States and the Arabic press indicate? This despite the fact that the *Protocols* had been legally and historically scrutinized and 'proven' to be a forgery early in the twentieth century. What do we make of Holocaust denial less than a half century after the Eichmann and Nuremberg trials were successful in holding accountable those who had committed war crimes and genocide? Even in the absence of a significant Jewish minority in many eastern European countries, the discourse of hate in the form of anti-Semitism is quite evident. Denise Roman writes that anti-Semitism in Romania, for instance, 'conveys an entire post-communist mythology, which constructs 'the Jew' as a 'mythical' fantasy, a representation symbolized by the idea of *an epicenter of international conspiracy against the nation*'.[6] Scholars write that the anti-Semitism of post-communist Europe is 'anti-Semitism without Jews'. For despite the drastically reduced numbers of Jews , especially in post-communist eastern Europe, the hated 'mythical Jew' has reappeared (or perhaps never really disappeared) in the form of hate speech and other hate crimes. While this is not a book about anti-Semitism per se, it is a book about the processes whereby history, law and the media are often implicated in its perpetuation.

Focusing on one of three sets of trials, *Protocols of the Elders of Zion*, Nuremberg/Eichmann or Holocaust Denial, each contributor to this volume ponders the reasons and ways in which anti-Semitism has persisted, despite historical and legal attempts to 'prove' the falsity of the underlying evidence gathered to perpetuate that hate, and the press's 'objective' reporting of such efforts. Each author takes up one or more issues critical to our understanding of the ways in which truth claims are made and the consequences of such claims. Despite the *Guardian*'s claim that 'History's Verdict on Holocaust Upheld',[7] each contributor cautions that truth is more than historical evidence, more than legal proofs and more than testimony and narrative. Not one takes for granted that the 'sheer weight of evidence' will assure truth's victory over racism or anti-Semitism. Whether one digs deep into the bowels of Auschwitz to unearth the truth (see van Pelt, Chapter 10), or assesses the political motivations of the USA during the Second World War to obfuscate the truth (see Feingold, Chapter 7) or one worries about the challenge of the use of testimony to reveal the truth (see Cole, Chapter 6), the truth is always embedded in many layers of reality, representation and perception. Not one author assumes an easy relationship with the way in which truth claims are made within their respective disciplines. Martha Minow, Professor of Law at Harvard University and author of *Between Vengeance and Forgiveness: Facing History After Genocide and Mass Violence* (1998), ruminates about the use of narratives and 'stories' to convince the courts about the truth or falsity of individual claims (see Minow, Chapter 5) and Fred Lawrence, Dean and Robert Kramer Research Professor of Law at George Washington University and author of *Punishing Hate: Bias Crimes Under American Law* (1999), points to how, under certain circumstances, one simply repeats the lie to tell the truth (see Lawrence, Chapter 4).

Clearly, evidence alone is not enough to change public opinion if one has a political stake in another interpretation. For instance, Stephen Bronner, Professor of Political Science and Comparative Literature at Rutgers University and author of *A Rumor about the Jews: Reflections on Antisemitism and the 'Protocols of the Learned Elders of Zion'* (2000), suggests that the authenticity of the *Protocols* should have been settled long before the last set of trials about it were scheduled. 'The fraud had already been uncovered by the middle of the 1920s,' he writes, 'since partisans of the pamphlet never produced an even marginally convincing explanation of how it was first discovered or a shred of evidence supporting its authenticity' (see Bronner, Chapter 2 p.20). Allan Ryan, Director, Office of Special Investigations, US Department of Justice, 1980–83 and author of *Quiet Neighbors: Prosecuting Nazi War Criminals in America* (1984), reflects on a similar point, but is alluding to Holocaust denial, when he notes that Associate Justice Jackson, the chief American prosecutor at the Nuremberg trials, proclaimed that after that trial there 'can be no responsible denial of these crimes in the future' (see Ryan, Chapter 9). While Ryan suggests to us why the Nuremberg trials have not prevented Holocaust denial, Laurel Leff, Professor of Journalism at Northeastern University and author of *Buried by the Times: The Holocaust and America's most Important Newspaper* (2005), focuses on the silences within media accounts about *both* the Nuremberg and the Eichmann trials. She writes of how ongoing frameworks prevented the press from addressing some of the key issues in understanding the Holocaust. Specifically, she refers to the press's reluctance during the Second World War to focus on the campaign to murder all of Europe's Jews. It would have, she reasons, required a new framework: 'Journalists would have had to acknowledge that the Germans were so determined to win the war against the Jews, they were willing to lose the war against America' (see Leff, Chapter 8 pp. 94–5).

Introducing the work of journalist Don Guttenplan into his essay, Tim Cole, Professor of Contemporary European Social and Cultural History at the University of Bristol, England, and author of *Selling the Holocaust* (1999), wrestles with the seeming conflict between testimony and the historical record, and what we do when the last survivor is gone. Guttenplan, writes Cole, suggest that 'without witnesses, without human voices to put flesh on the facts, we have something that, while it may pass muster as history, can never tell the truth' (see Cole, Chapter 6 p. 56). In his beautifully written and skillfully argued book, Dominic LaCapra makes clear that the ties between memory and history are tenuous.[8] Formulations of the meaning of the Holocaust, like all historical constructions, necessarily involve selectivity and judgment. As academicians, we know that there are often powerful conflicts within both the academy and the polity about whose selections and whose judgments dominate. James Young, Professor of Literature and Judaic Studies at the University of Massachusetts in Amherst, suggests how complicated our quest for truth can be when he writes that the

> contemporary critic can assert both the historicity of events and the crucial role interpretation played in the events themselves. This is not to deny the historical facts of the Holocaust outside of their narrative framing, but only to emphasize the difficulty of interpreting, expressing, and acting on these facts outside of the ways we frame them.[9]

The facts of history, as each author in this volume suggests, are always embedded in a social context, and therefore subject to the language and presentation of their times. Each contributor to this volume investigates the ways in which 'truth' is fashioned in the courtroom, in the court of public opinion and through historical analysis, as each explores one of three time periods (early, middle and late twentieth century) through one of three sets of trials (*Protocols of Zion*, Eichmann and Nuremberg, Lipstadt), from one of three different angles of vision: that of history, that of the press and that of the legal system.

The contributors to this book include some of the leading scholars, lawyers and journalists who, in the course of their own careers, have addressed issues of hate and hate crimes. Although he is referring to literary testimony, the following quote from James Young highlights a most important theme of our volume. He writes:

> Once we recognize that the 'facts' of history are not distinct from their reflexive interpretation in narrative, and that the 'facts' of the

Holocaust and their interpretation may even have been fatally interdependent, we are able to look beyond both the facts and the poetics of literary testimony to their consequences.[10]

The consequences, for history, the academy and the court of public opinion, are what we are about to explore here. However, before we turn to the chapters themselves, we will place them within an historical, media and legal framework.

HISTORY

The odd thing about coming to grips with historians' reactions to claims of anti-Semitism and Holocaust denial in the twentieth century is that the tools they adopted and utilized to refute such claims seem to have come full circle, as the century came to an end. For example, to combat the spurious claims of the *Protocols of the Elders of Zion* in the first three decades of the century, scholars utilized techniques of literary analysis to 'deconstruct' its sources (largely unrelated to anti-Semitism) and then to trace the processes of their plagiarism, perversion, assembly and dissemination. Their careful presentation of this 'history', based on close readings of the literary sources themselves and the testimony of witnesses to the forgery, succeeded in establishing the falsity both of the document itself and of the claims of an international Jewish conspiracy that derived from it. However, Bronner (see Chapter 2) concludes that neither the analyses nor the findings had any effect on its 'true-believers', because for them it had become an instant article of faith, an intuitive and a causal explanation for the confusing and frustrating modern world to which they believed they had fallen victim.

In the decade following the Second World War, the charges of 'Membership in a Criminal Organization' and 'Crimes Against Humanity' that Nazi officials and their collaborators faced at Nuremberg and elsewhere were designed, reports Henry Feingold (Professor of History and Director of the Jewish Resource Center at Baruch College and The Graduate Center, City University of NewYork) specifically to conceal the genocide perpetrated against the Jews (see Feingold, Chapter 7). The charges, although historically accurate, were placed within an obfuscatory universal framework, whose proof was to be derived mostly from around four thousand of the hundred thousand or so documents (textual, photographic and artifact) produced or preserved by the perpetrators themselves and captured by the Allies. These constituted what

British prosecution team member, Sir David Maxwell Fyfe, called 'the vast fortification of Nazi documents' (see Cole, Chapter 6 p.59) that future apologists would have to confront. Although some were called to testify, human 'witnesses' to the crimes (euphemistically referred to as 'displaced persons' in post-war parlance) were not only largely superfluous to the case, but would have forced the victors to confront awkward and troubling issues (such as past culpability and future settlement) that the victors wished to avoid (see Chapters 6, 8, and 9).

The appearance of Raul Hilberg's groundbreaking first edition of *The Destruction of the European Jews* in 1961 marked the full recognition of the centrality of the Jewish genocide to the Nazi program. However, the story of genocide was told largely from the documents of the perpetrators themselves. That same year, the Eichmann trial in Israel focused on these 'crimes against the Jewish people', but the evidence presented went beyond the documentary record to humanize the catastrophe by putting faces onto the victims (now characterized as heroes and martyrs), and began to shift the essential locus of the story from the perpetrators' documents to the testimony of 'survivors' and 'witnesses' (see Cole, Chapter 6). This 'paradigmatic shift' in the locus of 'truth telling', in Lawrence P. Douglas's words, from 'didactic [documentary]' to 'representational', served to spotlight the 'Holocaust' and the resistance that arose to it even under the most impossible of conditions (see Cole, Chapter 6).

The testimony heard in Jerusalem was not necessary to convict Eichmann. His own memoir, voluntarily written while in Israeli captivity and, paradoxically, released by the Israeli government as evidence refuting claims in the Irving suit, as well as the relevant Nuremberg documents, provided conclusive proof of his guilt. Since then, a veritable flood of survivor testimony has dominated the study of the Holocaust and has borne its 'truth' (see Cole, Chapter 6). When, in 1981, Mel Mermelstein answered the $50,000 challenge posted by the Legion for Survival of Freedom and the Institute for Historical Review to prove 'that Jews were gassed in gas chambers at Auschwitz' with the testimony of his own eyes and ears, he lost the challenge. When Mermelstein's subsequent suit caused a California 'court to take judicial notice of the fact that Jews were gassed to death at the Auschwitz Concentration Camp in Poland during the summer of 1944', it forced the denier organizations to settle out of court and to 'apologize ... for the pain, anguish, and suffering he and all other Auschwitz survivors have sustained relating to the challenge posted.'[11] The centrality of witness testimony to the 'truth' of the Holocaust seemed assured.

However, this avalanche of memory carried with it the frailty inherent in any witness testimony. The tie between memory and history is tenuous, since Holocaust memories were formed under conditions of terror and atrocity and subjected to the effects of trauma, age, distance, multiple retelling and continual (at least since 1978, when the NBC miniseries 'Holocaust' was broadcast) popular dramatization. In the wave of Holocaust denial, especially since the 1980s, every instance of confused, contradictory or falsified witness testimony (or testimony unsubstantiated by specific documentary confirmation), combined with decontextualized, misquoted or mistranslated documents, and specious technical or statistical analyses, were used to raise questions about the Holocaust itself and the guilt of its perpetrators. Reacting to the negative publicity that resulted, historians retreated from using testimony as a unique source for 'truth claims', to the more traditional documentary evidence on which narrative history has relied. When Deborah Lipstadt included David Irving among the deniers in her book, Irving sued Lipstadt for libel. Not wanting to subject the, by now, elderly survivors to Irving's vitriol, and concerned about the fragility of witness testimony, the Lipstadt defense team commissioned historians, such as Richard J. Evans, to sift through Irving's historical texts in search both of systematic bias and the improper use of documentary sources. More important, they commissioned van Pelt to sift through the concrete remains of Auschwitz to determine the 'truth' of Irving's claims concerning its destructive capacity and resources. Thus a combination of literary analysis, documentary research and physical examination provided the 'fortress' on which Irving's claims foundered.

Feingold writes that 'History may not be able to reveal the entire truth, but over time it is a great outer. It has taken time to piece together the tampered with historical record ... [b]ut each year, as the archives open wider, we learn more' (see Chapter 7 p. 76). History is never complete, never seamless, and never totally 'objective'. It builds its 'truth telling' by laboriously weaving together a wide array of evidence and interpretation. Historians interrogate archival material and human sources, not simply for their content or memories, but also for their documentary, geographic and historical contexts, their provenances, the reasons for their existence and survival and their resonance with other available materials or witnesses. Sometimes the juxtaposition of known, but previously unconnected, sources produces new insights. Sometimes new caches of materials are discovered or become available. Over time, through competing monographs, contentious conferences and critical reviews, historians cross-check one another's evidence, facts and documentation (as Evans and van Pelt did to Irving's work for the Lipstadt defense, later published respectively in 2001 as Richard J. Evans, *Lying About Hitler: History, Holocaust, and the David Irving Trial* and van Pelt, *The Case for Auschwitz: Evidence from the Irving Trial*) and reveal one another's interpretative frameworks, unconscious biases, evidentiary priorities, blind spots and standards of 'proof'. The process is not perfect. It can never reveal the past 'as it was', because too much concerning any period or event goes unrecorded. Differences in the meaning of the words or images or artifacts themselves cloud our comprehension even when the evidence exists. We cannot get inside protagonists' heads to distinguish motives from rationalizations. But this inter-subjective process does reveal ever more subtle contours of truth and the ability of the historical discipline to utilize theories, methodologies and insights from all areas of the study or expression of the human experience, allowing it to incorporate moral and aesthetic 'truths' into its own creative reconstruction.

THE MEDIA

Journalists often define their job as presenting the closest possible approximation of the truth. This implies that no one story, no one edition of a newspaper and no one broadcast, can attain the truth. This approximation of truth is developed within an interpretive framework shaped by media owners, public opinion, government policies, official sources, so-called experts, public relations and even propaganda. In examining media coverage of the *Protocols of the Elders of Zion*, Robert Hilliard, Professor of Media Arts at Emerson College and author of *Surviving the Americans: The Continued Struggle of the Jews After Liberation* (1997), shows us how some newspaper publishers, most prominently Henry Ford and his *Dearborn Independent*, promoted the Protocols as a vehicle for their anti-Semitism. Their failure to evaluate or even question the *Protocols* lent credence to one of history's most notorious fabrications. While Ford and others promoted the *Protocols*, most American journalists remained silent. Hilliard argues that Ford remains a hero for modern-day hatemongers, particularly on the Internet, where rumors and distortions are spread rapidly and anonymously. The legacy of the *Protocols*, writes Hilliard, remains with us (see Hilliard, Chapter 3).

A loosely defined set of journalistic norms continually evolve to shape the interpretive framework in which journalists work. News is generally considered something readers or listeners can relate to and what they seem to 'want' to know. News is usually close to home – geographically, culturally and emotionally. The interpretive framework that guides and shapes news is generated not only by the audience and by sources of information, but also by narrative techniques. These techniques have changed over time. In its early years, American journalism focused on anecdotes and the stories of individuals. By the end of the nineteenth century the model for news was the inverted pyramid, placing the most important facts at the beginning of a story. Most news stories consisted primarily of quotations from officials and from documents and events witnessed by individual reporters.

In her Chapter on the press's coverage of the Eichmann and Nuremberg trials, Leff shows that journalists downplayed the story of the extermination of the Jews (see Leff, Chapter 8). Their interpretations of these trials, she argues, were influenced by contemporary journalistic norms that focused on official actions and pronouncements, not on the experiences of individuals or victims. In covering the Nuremberg trials, Leff suggests that the press focused its attention on the most senior surviving German leaders. Because the extermination of the Jews did not feature prominently in the Nuremberg indictments, it was subsumed under a more general charge of 'crimes against humanity', the third of four charges. By the time the court even reached the crimes against humanity charge, late into the trial, press interest had already peaked. Therefore, in terms of both space and prominence, the Holocaust was only a footnote to an overpowering narrative at Nuremberg about aggressive war. The trials that more directly addressed the destruction of the Jews, such as that of the commandant and guards at Auschwitz and Bergen-Belsen, were considered of secondary importance. The *New York Times* –which ran a front-page story nearly every day about courtroom proceedings against the top German leaders – ran only two front-page stories on the trial of Auschwitz commandant Josef Kramer. Even this coverage tended to refer to the victims in general terms, or by their nationality. Only when a Jewish survivor testified and specifically mentioned the deaths of Jews were the victims referred to as Jews. As a result, writes Leff, the destruction of the Jews never emerged as a singular meaningful event (see Chapter 8).

In his presentation at the Northeastern University conference, Tom Segev argued that most journalists didn't consider either the

Mermelstein or Lipstadt trials worthy of coverage. From the journalist's perspective, he explains, the Holocaust denial at issue is an ugly phenomenon, but not particularly dangerous. Given the return among journalists during these trials to an earlier framework of storytelling and individual anecdotes, the predominant use of documentary evidence did not fit well. Indeed, argues Segev, extensive coverage of these trials might have served to bolster, rather than to repudiate, the deniers. It was insignificant for the history of the Holocaust, argues Segev, that a British judge has ruled that it actually happened. Segev suggests, instead, that the current wave of Holocaust denial and the widespread circulation of the *Protocols* in the Arab world, as opposed to the tiny minority of British and American deniers, is far more troubling and dangerous.

THE LAW

'Truth claims' do not fit comfortably with legal proceedings, although from a macro-perspective we hope that findings in legal proceedings have something to do with 'truth' and hence with 'justice'. The paradigm of a judicial proceeding in a civil suit, for instance, is a claim that the defendant has in some way wronged the plaintiff, or in a criminal suit, that the defendant is criminally responsible for some act. Either because some evidence is not directly relevant to these issues, or because, particularly in a criminal case, some of the evidence would be too prejudicial to the defendant, some evidence may be excluded. Two important differences emerge between the paradigm guiding legal proceedings and the work of a journalist or an academician. While all three disciplines direct their work towards a 'purpose', the cause of action in a legal proceeding is usually defined more narrowly. That is, much material that a journalist or an academic would find relevant and interesting towards the development of her work is often considered out of bounds in a legal proceeding.

Perhaps the greatest difference with respect to the handling of 'truth claims', however, flows from the concept of 'burden of proof'. Depending on the jurisdiction and the nature of the claim and its elements, either the plaintiff or the defendant will bear the burden of proving certain claims and/or elements (i.e., the burden of proof with respect to different elements can vary in the same case). Moreover, the burden of proof in most civil litigation is to convince either the judge or jury that the facts are more likely than not to have happened in the way they are presented ('preponderance of the evidence'), while the burden of proof in criminal litigation requires the prosecution to prove the elements of a crime 'beyond reasonable doubt'. Obviously, then, the fact that a judicial trial comes out one way or another does not really establish the 'truth' in any real sense, but simply means that the party bearing the burden of proof has not sustained that burden. While both the journalist and academician have 'standards' defined by their professions, these standards provide less constraint on what may be asserted as fact than the finding in a judicial proceeding that one's burden of proof has not been satisfied.

All of the above become even more complicated when we move beyond the simple paradigm of litigation to trials that are 'political', like those covered in this book. A trial can, of course, turn political even though its essence corresponds to the usual paradigm of litigation. For example, rather than focusing on early twentieth century litigation that concerned the *Protocols*, we might have chosen to focus on the Dreyfus trial. However, the Dreyfus trial only turned political because of the religious affiliation of the defendant and the circumstances under which he was tried. The alleged act (the conveying of military secrets to a potential enemy) was not political in the sense of trying to prove or disprove a political event or writing. To take another example, the O. J. Simpson trial only became political because an African American was accused of killing his white wife, and the defense made race an issue. The fact that Simpson was acquitted did not mean that the 'truth claim' of his innocence was established. Rather, it meant simply that the prosecution had not borne its burden of establishing Simpson's guilt in the eyes of the jury. A lesser burden and/or a different jury (as the subsequent civil trial indicated) might have resulted in a different verdict.

Given the above distinctions, let us be more specific about the litigation that we are exploring in this volume. If, for instance, in the set of trials of the *Protocols of the Elders of Zion*, had the Detroit litigation not been settled or the Swiss litigation not been successful, would judicial findings of 'no liability' have meant that the *Protocols* constituted a genuine document? Hardly – it simply would have meant that the plaintiffs in those cases failed to bear their burdens of proof. Similarly, suppose that Mermelstein or Lipstadt had lost and the Institute for Historical Review and Irving had won. Would, for instance, an Irving 'win' have meant that Auschwitz did not have gas chambers and that Jews had largely fabricated and exaggerated the Shoah? Of course not – it simply would have meant that Lipstadt had not borne her burden of proof.

We have rightly asked the question of what outside influences and pressures affect the legal process, particularly if we are speaking about litigation and trials having the political dimensions of the three sets of litigation with which this volume is concerned. The short answer is that judges are people, who read the same newspapers, while drinking their morning coffee, as do others. It was unlikely, then, that the judges and prosecutors at Nuremberg, most especially the chief American prosecutor, Associate Justice Jackson, would not have convicted the accused of 'war crimes'. And, despite the burdens placed on the defendant in the Irving/ Lipstadt trial, there was little doubt that the judge would ultimately hold against Irving. The question of whether, and with what consistency, judges can withstand the popular prejudice that *corresponds* with what they read in the newspapers is a different question (see Chapters 4, 5 and 9 for further expansion on these points).

CONCLUSION

We wish to end this introduction with a caution that James Young might have added, had a last minute emergency not prevented him from attending the conference. The concern that each of us has, in Young's words, is that once we locate meaning and the representation of truth within its own sociohistoric framework, we leave ourselves with the 'hypothetical possibility' that events and the many ways those events are re-presented (for instance, as narrative, as historical record, as judicial proof, as testimonial, as memory) 'never existed outside each other and that all meanings of events created in different representations are only relative'.[12] Not one author or editor wishes to leave the reader with the notion that truth is relative and therefore all claims are equally valid, a consequence often associated with the postmodern turn in so many fields and disciplines. We do not wish to obscure, but to illuminate, the 'inevitable interpenetration'[13] of law, history and the media in framing the ways in which we interpret, express and act upon historical events. Our task in this volume is not to 'prove' that the *Protocols* are a forgery, or that crimes against humanity and genocide against the Jewish people occurred. The *Protocols* are a forgery and crimes against humanity and genocide against the Jewish people did happen. Our task is rather to mark the ways – conscious, unconscious, malevolent, honorable – in which we present and re-present the historical facts, the journalism and the legal proofs that undergird the truth of those assertions.

Debra Renee Kaufman, Professor of Sociology and Matthews Distinguished University Professor, Northeastern University, Boston,

MA.

Gerald Herman, Director of Interdisciplinary Studies and Assistant Professor of History and Education, Northeastern University, Boston, MA.

David Phillips, Professor of Law, Northeastern University, Boston, MA.

James Ross, Stotsky Professor of Jewish Historical and Cultural Studies and Associate Professor of Journalism, Northeastern University, Boston, MA.

NOTES

1. Irving based his conclusions on the work of Fred A. Leuchter, who argued that there were no homicidal gas chambers at Auschwitz. Van Pelt's macabre task – discussed in chapter 10 –was to show systematically that there was indeed architectural evidence that Auschwitz could and did serve the function of a gas chamber for the murder of Jews.
2. *Atlantic Monthly*, February 2000, p. 45.
3. Robert Jan van Pelt, *The Case for Auschwitz: Evidence from the Irving Trial.* (Boomington: Indiana University, 2002), p. x.
4. Ibid., p. xi.
5. This is a quote from the *Guardian* cited by van Pelt, ibid.
6. Denise Roman, *Fragmented Identities: Popular Culture, Gender, and Everyday Life in Post-Communist Romania* (Lanham, MD: Lexington Books, 2003), p. 84.
7. Cited in van Pelt, *Case for Auschwitz* (Bloomington: Indiana University Press, 2002), p. xi.
8. LaCapra, Dominic, *History and Memory after Auschwitz* (Ithaca, NY: Cornell University Press, 1998).
9. James Young, *Writing and Rewriting the Holocaust* (Yale University Press, 1988).
10. Ibid., p. 39.
11. Superior Court of the State of California for the County of Los Angeles, No. C 356542, 5 August 1985, Robert A. Wenke, Judge; Statement of Record and Letter of Apology dated 24 August 1985.
12. Young, p. 3.
13. Ibid.

2

Libeling the Jews: Truth Claims, Trials, and the Protocols of Zion

STEPHEN ERIC BRONNER

> When things as clear as this need to be proved, you are sure to convince no one.'
> – Montesquieu

The *Protocols of the Learned Elders of Zion* was not the first document to libel the Jews. But it is surely the most famous or, better, infamous.[1] The tract comprises the minutes from 24 sessions of a congress supposedly held by representatives from the 'twelve tribes of Israel', and led by a Grand Rabbi in a cemetery under a full moon, whose apparent purpose was to articulate the plan for Jewish world conquest. Inspired by the radicalizing impact of the Dreyfus Affair, and the First Zionist Congress that took place in 1897 under the leadership of Theodor Herzl, the *Protocols* first appeared in Russia in 1903 on a single sheet that could be pasted on a wall. In 1905, however, a more complete version appeared as the appendix to *The Great in the Small: The Coming of the Antichrist and the Rule of Satan on Earth*, written by the half-crazed Russian religious fanatic, Sergei Nilus, who longed to become a spiritual adviser to the czar.

The *Protocols* were initially employed to blame the Jews and their supposed allies, the Freemasons, for the 1905 Revolution. But it soon proved adaptable to other situations when it was spread abroad by 'white' exiles following their defeat by the 'reds' in the Russian civil war. The American version of 1920 claimed that a larger plan for destroying the republic underlay the 'Jewish' role in the 'Black Sox' baseball scandal of 1921, while the South African variant maintained that the Talmud and Torah commanded Jews to make non-Jews drink their urine and eat their vomit. The Nazis saw its value immediately, and the Patriarch of Jerusalem called on his followers to purchase the Arabic translation in 1925. Its condemnation of the Jewish threat was echoed in the 1930s by populist demagogues such as Father Charles Coughlin, while General Francisco Franco used the *Protocols* to justify a rebellion against the existing republic that would save the 'true Spain' from anarchists, atheists, communists and a 'Judeo-Masonic conspiracy'. Even today the *Protocols* have been the subject of an anti-Semitic television pseudo-documentary, 'Rider without a Horse', in Egypt and it has been republished in Tunisia, Iraq, Iran and elsewhere in the Arab world. Every version, however, makes the same point regarding Jewish intentions for world conquest and the destruction of Christian civilization.

Perhaps other works had already reduced the struggle over modernity to the ongoing conflict between Jews and Gentiles,[2] but none so starkly or dramatically as the *Protocols*. The pamphlet both expresses and reinforces an already existing prejudice. But it also offers an explanation of human history particularly appropriate for those threatened by the progressive ideas and movements usually associated with the Enlightenment and the 'age of democratic revolution'. The first protocol, in fact, lets the Grand Rabbi say that: 'we were the first to cry among the masses of the people the words *liberty, equality, fraternity*'. The Jew is portrayed as the agent of modernity and the destroyer of traditions associated with the closed homogeneous community, the autarkic economy, the divinely sanctioned aristocracy and the church. Indeed, the tenth protocol notes how the Jews will use 'dissension, hatred, struggle, envy and even the use of torture', starvation, and the willingness to spread disease, in order to throw the Christian world into chaos and to achieve their goal of world conquest.

The *Protocols* are basically a distorted plagiarism of a relatively unknown republican work titled *A Dialogue in Hell: Conversations Between Montesquieu and Machiavelli about Power and Justice* (1864) by Maurice Joly, coupled with, in various editions, the setting in the cemetery culled from the anti-Semitic novel *Biarritz* (1868) by Hermann Goedsche. But the pamphlet is none the less a seminal contribution to what was an established anti-Semitic intellectual and political tradition. It crystallizes in simple fashion the connections among its religious, social and political aspects, the three components *always* encoded in anti-Semitic theory and practice. It also provides a glimpse into what makes anti-Semitism unique among the various forms of group hatred: it presents the Jew as what I have called a *chameleon*, and the strength of the ideology is the extent to which the *chameleon effect* is in operation.[3]

Other forms of prejudice may identify the enemy with certain stereotypes, but these are relatively fixed. Racists may consider people of color genetically inferior to whites and a drain on public finances, for example, but they don't simultaneously claim that people of color control capital and the media. Even a cursory reading of the *Protocols*, however, reveals that the Jew is not simply the homosexual, or the avant-garde bohemian, the capitalist, or the communist revolutionary. Stereotyping takes a new form in this pamphlet: the Jew is now *any* enemy required by the anti-Semite. And suddenly, this enemy will change shape. The Jew thereby becomes invisible – only his impact is palpable. The twelfth protocol, in this vein, likens the Jew to the Indian idol Vishnu, whose hundred hands each controls a different newspaper, party and organ of public opinion with an eye on common, if hidden, Jewish interests. The chameleon effect takes a particularly radical form in the *Protocols* and it has radical, if unarticulated implications. Precisely because the Jew is everywhere and controls everything, invisible and ubiquitous, the anti-Semite is left with only one sensible option: annihilation of the Jew and the all-encompassing Jewish conspiracy. Indeed, if only for this reason, it was necessary to take the *Protocols* seriously.

The best-known attack on the pamphlet was launched in 1933 when the Jewish community of Berne sued Georg Bernhard Haller, editor-in-chief of the Nazi-oriented paper *Confederates of the Oath* (*Eidgenossen*), and its publisher, Theodor Fischer, for libel and distributing 'smut literature' (*Schundliteratur*).[4] Also named in the suit were Theodor Fritsch and Gottfried zur Beek, the German editor of the tract, who died before the trial began. Other individuals accused of affirming the truth of the *Protocols* included Silvio Schnell, who served as its Swiss editor, and finally, the prominent architect and member of the National Front, Walter Aebersold. All of them immediately disclaimed any personal responsibility, and in a way, they were irrelevant to the proceedings. The real enemies were the Swiss National Front, the Union of Swiss National Socialists, and most importantly, their sponsor – German Nazism.

The Berne trial began in the last week in October 1934. Officially, the Nazi state refused to intervene. But that did not prevent it from employing the fiercely anti-Semitic publicist, Ulrich Fleischhauer, to organize support for the defendants. Even while the domestic strategy was initially left in the hands of Ubald von Roll, the official leader of the

Berne section of the Swiss National Front, and his deputy Boris Todtli, Fleischhauer increasingly took charge of the proceedings and his 'expert' report to the court on the 'inner truth' of the *Protocols* became an anti-Semitic classic. Nevertheless, from the first, the defendants found themselves in a seemingly untenable situation: they had to authenticate what they knew was a fraudulent document.

The defendants chose not to call witnesses of their own, and instead concentrated on demeaning the plaintiffs and their supporters. They could not prove any relationship between the Jews and the Freemasons, nor could they produce any evidence capable of substantiating the authenticity of the *Protocols* or of discrediting the evidence brought by the other side. They became enmeshed in different versions of how the *Protocols* came into existence. Maintaining that Maurice Joly was actually born a Jew named Moishe Joel, they had little to say when his birth certificate was entered into evidence. Questioned on the claim by Goedsche that the twelve tribes of Israel had met to plan world domination, they were dumbfounded when it was noted that only the tribes of Judah and Benjamin had survived the destruction of the Second Temple in AD 70. After claiming that the minutes of the First Zionist Congress were the origin of the *Protocols*, they could not explain why stenographed copies had not been drafted in German, which was the official language of the congress. Indeed, when the new 1934 edition of the *Protocols* was published in Leipzig by the Hammer Verlag, its editor abandoned this standard view and insisted instead that it was the record of a 'secret meeting' of the B'nai B'rith, the Jewish community service organization. And so it went. Basically, the arguments of the defense boiled down to a tautology: the *Protocols* should be seen as authentic because the Jews are evil, and the Jews are evil because the pamphlet says so.[5]

The only hope for the defense was to turn the trial for libel into a political event. To this end, they employed traditional fascist tactics: they disrupted the proceedings, intimidated witnesses, and threatened to counter-sue the Jewish community for libel. They asked questions regarding why the Jews had no homeland and they falsified claims about Jewish rituals. They challenged witnesses by highlighting their political affiliations, and impugned experts with wild accusations about their moral character. They claimed that Jews could not speak the truth and that the trial was controlled by the Jewish conspiracy. They insisted it was impossible for the defenders of the Aryan race to get justice when faced with such a powerful and organized Jewish opposition. They maintained that the trial was not really about the veracity or falsity of the *Protocols* at all, but rather the 'inner truth' it represented.

The Jewish plaintiffs, on the other hand, were intent on demonstrating the *Protcols* lack of authenticity and the outlandish character of their claims. The legal team was composed of a few historians and leaders of the Swiss Jewish community, and led by Georges Brunschvig. It was short on funds and friends. But the plaintiffs could rely on experts like Arthur Baumgarten and Carl Loosli, a popular Swiss author of *The Bad Jews!* and an expert on the *Protocols*, as well as on important Russian historians and former political figures like Boris Nicolayevsky and Paul Miliukov. They employed the testimony of Armand du Chayla, a former friend of Nilus, who had personal knowledge of the fabrication, along with figures like Chaim Weizmann, President of the World Zionist Organization, and Dr Markus Ehrenpreis, Chief Rabbi of Stockholm, who could speak on the lack of foundation for any notion of a 'world conspiracy' in either the Jewish religion or Zionism.

On 14 May 1935 the verdict was delivered. The judge, Walter Meyer, a practicing Christian who had previously never heard of the *Protocols*, found in favor of the plaintiffs. He stated unambiguously that the pamphlet was a forgery and a work of plagiarism; he considered it libelous and a perfect example of 'smut literature' that deserved to be banned as incendiary. The Nazis appealed and, unfortunately, the Swiss Court of Appeal found the definition of 'smut literature' to be identical with sexual pornography under Swiss law. Although the *Protocols* may well be obscene, or so the argument went, it is not obscene in a pornographic sense. Thus, in November 1937, the court overturned the earlier judgment for formal reasons, while at the same time confirming the previous finding that the *Protocols* was a fabrication and constituted smut literature in a general sense. The two decisions mirror the dichotomy in the heart of Switzerland during the 1930s.

More generally, however, the trial showed that Hitler and his friends were correct in their original assessment: it was never simply a fight for the truth, but rather 'an attempt to fuse the mechanical elements of the political trial outside the atmosphere of constitutional government – the comfortable but unproductive certainty of the result – with the creation of a political imagery appropriate for present needs'.[6] The question is to what extent this aim was realized. The specific arguments employed by either side in their attempts to justify or distort truth claims consequently becomes secondary, and it is somehow fitting that the arguments concerning the *Protocols* – both pro and con – should have offered little that was new. What was truly at stake had already become clear by the end of 1937. Those who had chosen to vacillate, whether from fear or opportunism, would continue to vacillate. The minds of both fascists and antifascists had been made up long before. The trial made clear the contradictory situation in which Jewish plaintiffs always find themselves when dealing with the charges of the anti-Semite in a public forum: those willing to recognize the truth need no convincing, while those in need of convincing will never allow themselves to recognize the truth or, for that matter, the legitimacy of the independent judicial arena in which it is being determined.

None of this is obviously meant to deny the efforts undertaken by the Jews of Switzerland and elsewhere to discredit the *Protocols* and to dispel the myths justifying anti-Semitism. But the fact remains that the Swiss trial begs questions concerning both the enduring appeal of this ideology and the ways of contesting it. Issues concerning the authenticity of the *Protocols* should, in principle, have been settled long before the trial began. The fraud had already been uncovered by the middle of the 1920s, since partisans of the pamphlet had never once produced an even marginally convincing explanation of how it was first discovered, or a shred of evidence supporting its authenticity, or had demonstrated the existence of a group known as the 'elders of Zion,' let alone a Grand Rabbi, or any plan for world conquest by the Jewish people. Today, it is particularly important to draw a distinction between Israeli policy toward the Palestinians and a Jewish conspiracy intent upon ruling the world, if only because working with wrongheaded assumptions inevitably leads to wrongheaded politics. But there is a way in which none of this really has any impact on the person psychologically inclined toward bigotry. It is for the anti-Semite less a matter of whether the *Protocols* are authentic, than whether they accurately portray what can be intuited about 'Jewish' intentions.

In this regard, when seen sociologically, anti-Semitism has always had greater appeal for some groups than for others. During the 1920s, for example, it appealed to war veterans, incapable of dealing with civilian existence or of making sense of the apocalypse they had just barely survived, along with youths of good upbringing stripped of their prospects for a decent life. In Europe, however, the most receptive audience for anti-Semitic ideology has generally been the stalwarts of the provincial 'community': aristocrats incapable of realizing that their time is past, the peasantry and the small shopkeepers disoriented by modern forms of production, the low-level bureaucrats with 'connections' intent on justifying their position, and the dregs of the industrial metropolis ready to express their resentment through violence. These groups constituted the mass base for European fascism, and many of them still serve as core clientele for the Nation of Islam, the Klu Klux Klan and the right-wing militias in the United States. They are the losers left behind by modernity. The same can be said for the Palestinians, but with a twist. For them the Jews are *not* an invisible threat.[7] The *Protocols*, despite their popularity in much of the Middle East and their underground appeal in the West, no longer have anything like the appeal they did in the 1920s and 1930s when they were – after the Bible – the most read document in the world. There is nothing more dangerous than attempting to blend the experience of times past with the reality of a new millennium.

To be sure, economic crisis can clearly prove an important factor in increasing the popularity of anti-Semitism among the 'losers', and the Weimar Republic served as a case in point. Anti-Semitism is, however, not mechanically reducible to economic interests. Neither the United States nor England ever had a 'Jewish problem' comparable to that of continental European nations during the twentieth century, although they, too, went through the Great Depression. The most important reason, I think, lies in the strength of their liberal institutions and, just as importantly, of the democratic traditions embedded in their civic culture. In continental Europe, the situation was far simpler: it was precisely in countries whose republican institutions suffered a crisis of legitimacy, and in which ideological conflict between the partisans and the critics of Enlightenment traditions resulted in a national identity crisis, that anti-Semitism became a matter of profound concern.

This only makes sense given the way in which anti-Semitism has been rooted in western civilization. It never constituted an independent impulse, but was rather always interconnected with the struggle to resist the new, the civilizing impulse of reason and the increasing complexity of modern life. Old fears can be experienced in new ways by those who have lost faith in the ability of progressive forces to deal with the problems of modern life. Important too is the way in which pessimism rather than optimism about the future inflames the fanaticism of the bigot. Indeed, precisely because resistance against this all-powerful Jewish conspiracy increasingly presents itself as a losing proposition, the anti-Semite can be seen as suffering from a peculiar form of paranoia, inflamed by an intense sense of urgency concerning the impending collapse of Christian civilization.

The situation has today been somewhat changed in the Middle East, where the old prejudice is bound up with the actual grievances of dispossessed Palestinians desperately in need of redress, the attempts by dictatorial Arab states to deflect the oppression of their own peoples by making reference to a traditional 'scapegoat', and the attempts by Israeli politicians to identify criticism of Israel with anti-Semitism. The plight of the losers and their resentment cannot simply be dismissed just as attempts to manipulate the past, and the bigotry experienced in the past cannot simply be ignored. At this time it might be better to begin thinking about building bridges between the Jewish experience of the past and the Palestinian experience of the present.

Anti-Semitism of the sort promoted by the *Protocols* cannot help matters: it is merely the stupid answer to a serious question. Its importance lies only in forcing us to confront not simply the bigotry but its sources, or, expressed another way, the perverse *ratio* of the *irratio* of the anti-Semite. The *Protocols* illuminate the ideological resistance to the Enlightenment foundations of modernity, and privilege intuitive prejudice over reasoned argument and myth over empirical evidence. They show just how insightful Jean-Paul Sartre was when he termed anti-Semitism a 'passion' that turns the bigot into 'stone'.[8] Making the 'choice to reason falsely', according to this great proponent of existentialism, the anti-Semite embraces bigotry because its simple explanation of human affairs *unequivocally* affirms his or her original intuition in every instance. Or, put differently, the truth of the anti-Semitic claim, or so the anti-Semite assumes, is self-evident, and if it is not recognized as such, then it is because of the 'intellectual' confusion sown by the Jews. The ideology offers not merely a scapegoat, in this respect, but a peculiar form of existential security or, better, insularity from criticism. This individual is consequently never wrong – which has its appeal.

Anti-Semites pay the price for always being in the right by choosing to exist less as individual subjects than as objects threatened by a dark conspiracy. This enables them not only to avoid taking responsibility, but also to justify their own dogmatic and authoritarian convictions by identifying them with Jewish intentions. The paranoid personality always engages in a form of projection, and this kind of psychological mechanism is clearly evidenced in the *Protocols*. The Jews are supposedly willing to employ all available means to bring about the destruction of Christian – or Islamic – civilization, therefore anti-Semites must immediately employ all available means to bring about the destruction of the Jews. The Jew supposedly controls public opinion, therefore, the anti-Semite must immediately insist on the control of public opinion. The Jew is supposedly engaged in an all-powerful conspiracy, therefore, The anti-Semite must immediately enter into his or her own conspiracy in order to fight this all-powerful foe.

The *Protocols* never provides a concrete analysis of any particular situation. Conflicts and differences among Jews are lost, their traditions become reified into an imaginary plot, and the strategy directed against them becomes defined by authoritarianism, bigotry and a refusal to look at the real political world of constraints and opportunities. The anti-Semite becomes defined by his own Jewish construct. Paranoia breeds the bigot's sense of urgency, and the sense of urgency intensifies his or her paranoia. The illusory insight into the existence of a Jewish conspiracy, by the same token, allows the anti-Semitic loser to understand himself as 'normal' – admittedly although in an exaggerated way. The martyr to the destabilizing forces of modern life can now serve as the champion of traditional values like family, church, nation and community. Anti-Semitism from the existential standpoint of the anti-Semite consequently provides an entry pass into respectable society. If other members of the community don't recognize the looming threat emanating from the Jews, because they are blinded by the sophistries of Jewish rationalism, then all the better. This only further justifies the original paranoia: it legitimates the condemnation of those gentiles supposedly duped by the conspiracy, the self-perception of the anti-Semite as the persecuted prophet and the increasing urgency of the message.

Anti-Semitism can be understood as the philosophy of those who choose to think with their gut. Its claims rest on *faith*: the point is not whether they are true, but whether the anti-Semite *believes* them to be true. Hence the danger of exaggerating the educational impact of purely legal proceedings, simple empirical proof, or the purely analytic justification of truth claims. It is important, then, to also focus on thet *style of thinking* in which rumor and the myth, intuition and 'felt' experience, become the *only* necessary justifications for truth claims. This calls for thinking about the type of institutions beyond the republican state that are conducive to the exercise of reason and tolerance in civil society. In spite of the tensions existing between different minorities, and their divergent attempts to privilege their particular historical experiences of suffering and persecution, such a commitment might be the first step in linking the battle against anti-Semitism with the larger battle against bigotry in general.

NOTES

1. All references to the *Protocols* are taken from the selections provided in Stephen Eric Bronner,

A Rumor about the Jews: Anti-Semitism, Conspiracy, and the 'Protocols of Zion' (New York: Oxford University Press, 2004), pp. 11–31.
2. Norman Cohn, *Warrant for Genocide: The Myth of the Jewish World Conspiracy and the Protocols of the Elders of Zion* (London: Eyre & Spottiswoode, 1967).
3. Bronner, *Rumor about the Jews*, pp. 145–6.
4. This best analysis of this trial is offered by Hadassa Ben-Itto, *The Lie That Wouldn't Die: The Protocols of the Elders of Zion* (London: Vallentine Mitchell, 2005), Chapter 11.
5. A pamphlet claiming that the trial actually proved the assertions made by the defendants about the Jews was published by Karl Bergmeister, *Der judische Weltverschworungsplan: Die Protokolle der Weissen von Zion vor dem Strafgerichte in Bern* (1937). The first postwar edition, was distributed by White Power Publications (Liverpool, West VA, 1977).
6. Otto Kirchheimer, *Political Justice: The Use of Legal Procedure for Political Ends* (Princeton, NJ: Princeton University Press, 1961), pp. 105.
7. Stephen Eric Bronner, 'States of Despair: History, Politics, and Resistance in Palestine', *in Blood in th Soul: Imperial Fantasies, Right-Wing Ambitions and the Erosion of American Democracy* (Lexington: University of Kentucky, 2005) pp. 60 ff. Also see the discussion of my book on the *Protocols*, 'Rumors and Reflections: A Reply to Dean Ian Markham', *Conversations in Religion and Theology* (Fall, 2004), p.206 ff..
8. Jean-Paul Sartre, *Anti-Semite and Jew* (trans. George Becker; New York: Schocken Books, 1948), pp. 10, 18.

3

The Media and the Holocaust: Protocols of the Elders of Zion – Then and Now

ROBERT L. HILLIARD

In George Bernard Shaw's play *The Devil's Disciple*, British General Burgoyne laments to his aide that England will lose the colonies because a clerk in the home office in London let Burgoyne's dispatch, which urgently requested that additional troops be sent immediately, sit for several days on his desk because of his eagerness to leave for the weekend.

'What will history say?' the aide asks in dismay.
'History, Sir,' Burgoyne answers, 'will tell lies as usual.'

I flew to this conference from Fort Myers, Florida, where Thomas Edison's winter home and laboratory and Henry Ford's neighboring winter estate are principal tourist attractions. The tour guide discusses at length Ford and Edison's work and their close friendship. At no point is Ford's virulent anti-Semitism mentioned; nor is his worldwide distribution of the *International Jew* or the *Protocols of the Learned Elders of Zion*, both key factors in the exacerbation of the anti-Semitism in Europe that facilitated the cooperation of most countries, most people, and most lay and religious institutions and organizations with the Holocaust of the Second World War. The media have convinced America to honor Edison and his close friend, Ford – a bigot who helped facilitate the murder of millions – as heroes.

History tells us what the rich and powerful want it to tell us. We've made progress in the past century-plus, since the *Protocols of Zion* first began its nefarious influence on the worldwide public. Or have we? Let's look briefly at some of the impact of the *Protocols* on society then – and now. One of our purposes in this book is to discuss the impact of legal actions involving the *Protocols*, including the trial in Switzerland that concluded, in court findings in Berne in 1935, that the German edition of the *Protocols*, first published in 1919, was a fake and a forgery. What is perhaps even more important is that the *Protocols* themselves generated other trials – trials that implemented the purposes behind the exploitation of the *Protocols*.

A prime example of this is the oft-cited trial of Mendel Bellis in czarist Russia in 1913. Bellis, a Jew, was tried for allegedly committing ritual murder in 1911 in order to obtain Christian blood for a Passover celebration. This was an accusation frequently made about Jews and attributed to the *Protocols*. Like the title of Stephen Bronner's book, *A Rumor About the Jews*, it was one of many widely accepted rumors. Indeed, when the Lindbergh baby was kidnapped and murdered in the early 1930s, some anti-Semitic groups alleged that the deed was done by Jews to obtain Christian blood for Passover. Aside from the fact that there was no evidence linking Bellis to the murder of the 13-year-old male victim, the Kiev authorities used the case to justify increased anti-Jewish pogroms in Russia, fueled by the distribution of the *Protocols of Zion*, allegedly by the Okhrana, the Czar's secret police. As an aside, I might note that I am here today only because my father, at the age of 16, said goodbye to his family and fled Russia in 1910 to escape a pogrom. I expect that something similar exists in the background of many others – our lives completely affected, even thousands of miles and many decades away, by the *Protocols*.

Despite a handpicked jury, a viciously anti-Semitic trial judge and a parade of lying prosecution witnesses, Bellis was found innocent. But the purpose of the trial was realized: the jury concluded that a ritual murder to obtain Christian blood for the Jewish Passover did occur. This was a victory for the *Protocols*! How many more trials, stimulating the mounting anti-Semitism that led to the Holocaust, did the *Protocols of Zion* facilitate?

The media, by their overt support of or silence about the book and its claims, promoted the purposes of those who exploited the *Protocols*. Media approaches were similar to those of today: media owners decide on the basis of their personal beliefs (and prejudices) what is fit to print. And like the contemporary mass media, newspapers at the time were influenced by advertisers – immensely powerful corporate entities dedicated to maintaining the status quo or to moving the world's social and environmental development backwards. In other countries – the United Kingdom being one of the exceptions – the press was, and usually is controlled by the government in power, whether by direct ownership or by control of the content of the privately owned media through a specified government ministry. Yet even in the UK, the rich, powerful or famous could have their beliefs made manifest in the media. For example, Winston Churchill, writing for the *Illustrated Sunday Herald*, helped to legitimize the *Protocols* story with his comments about Jews.[1]

Therefore, in large part, the promotion of, or at least the lack of objective evaluation of the *Protocols*, was the policy of many governments and of the press, and the book was and continues to be published in many countries and in many languages. The *Protocols* were even used openly as a rationale by the United States Congress to pass harshly restrictive immigration laws. Keep in mind that media owners were and still are, in large part, close to the leaders of their respective governments and are powerful lobbying forces even in democratic societies.

I return to Henry Ford, as one of those powerful people whose particular hate – in this case anti-Semitism – could be used to fuel genocide anywhere in the world. Despite the *New York Times*'s condemnation of the *Protocols of Zion* in 1920 as 'the strangest jumble of crazy ideas that ever found its way into print',[2] a series of virulent anti-Semitic articles in Ford's newspaper, the *Dearborn Independent*, based in large part on the *Protocols*, were published as the *International Jew*. Along with the *Protocols of Zion*, Ford distributed it internationally, focusing on Germany. These Ford-supported books strongly aided Hitler's campaign against the Jews from the 1920s onward. Holocaust scholar Norman Cohn has called the *Protocols* a 'warrant for genocide'.[3]

Ford is hailed as a hero of American ingenuity and a great patriot who spurred the economic growth of his country. With the exception of historians and Holocaust scholars, few people know that Adolf Hitler kept a large portrait of Henry Ford on a wall in his private office[4] and was known to have stated that he regarded Henry Ford as his inspiration. Hitler lauded Ford for distributing the *Protocols of the Elders of Zion*, believing that every word of it describing a Jewish conspiracy to destroy Christian civilization and take over the world was true, and he awarded Ford the Grand Cross of the German Eagle. Hitler also stated that 'we look to Heinrich Ford as the leader of the growing Fascist movement in America.'[5] At one point in the early 1920s Ford temporarily withdrew overt support of the *Protocols*, for business purposes, but continued his anti-Semitism through innuendo and not very well-hidden code words. In 1924 the *Dearborn Independent* resumed its vicious anti-Semitic attacks and in 1927 it was sued for libel by Aaron Sapiro – a lawyer who had been working with farm cooperatives that Ford disliked – a libel that linked Sapiro with 'Jewish combination', 'international banking rings' and 'Jewish international bankers'. The proceedings ended in a mistrial: Ford's lawyers were found to have been intimidating jurors. A few months later Ford issued a long apology for the newspaper's anti-Semitism, claiming he had known nothing about it.

Bu when the Second World War erupted, Ford proclaimed that 'Jew bankers' had instigated it. Further, the American Ford Company not only permitted, but abetted its German subsidiaries in the production of vehicles for the Nazi military prior to the USA's involvement in the war in 1941. It arranged for the Nazis to receive vast amounts of strategic war materials and even after America became involved in the war, American Ford received a dividend from a German subsidiary in Cologne that employed forced labor.[6]

I concentrate on Ford as more than a symbol. He was and is a national hero; he was the friend and confidante of almost every political and industrial leader. How better to inform the public about the true nature of sacred cows, about the ease with which the *Protocols* and anti-Semitism invade our national weal, than by putting Henry Ford on trial, even now?

It is important that we study the history of the *Protocols of Zion* – but not for the purpose of historical analysis or discussion. The primary purpose should be to prevent others from recreating history. Many scholars of the *Protocols* have suggested that its time has passed, that it has so often been shown to be fraudulent that few pay attention to it today, that its impact on society has greatly decreased and is, in fact, negligible. Unfortunately, they are wrong. Throughout the world, even in so-called enlightened countries such as France, new editions of the *Protocols of the Elders of Zion* sell extensively. Their impact is so strong that a number of Arab leaders vitiate the legitimate elements of condemning the Israeli government's policy toward Palestinians by quoting from the *Protocols*.

The legacy of the *Protocols* exists in the United States today. The classic book on their history and influence, *A Lie and a Libel*, notes that in the late 1920s 'the *Protocols* found a home among fundamentalist Christian and right-wing anticommunist organizations'.[7] While researching and writing our 1999 book, *Waves of Rancor: Tuning in the Radical Right*, co-author Michael Keith and I found that the *Protocols* and the hate they spawned were very much alive, and constructed one of the motivating forces for the millions of members of hate groups in the United States and throughout the world today. We need only look at a few of the approximately 2,000 hate sites on the Internet in the USA alone to see the *Protocols* in action.

Bronner writes that 'the central idea of the *Protocols* involves the supposed Jewish world conspiracy designed to enslave Christian civilization under a new world order run by the leading elder of Zion.'[8] Perhaps the strongest unifying factor among present-day hate groups is the belief that Jewish leaders in Israel, using their control of the United Nations, are proceeding with their plans – as revealed in the *Protocols* – to establish a New World Order that will take over America and destroy the white Christian race.

To counter this, right-wing extremists openly proclaim their goals for a racial holy war against Jews, people of color, homosexuals, Catholics, pro-choice advocates, and others who disagree with their philosophies and goals. As the FBI has warned us, neo-Nazi, Christian identified, radical armed militias, white supremacist and other hate organizations are arming for such an Armageddon. Many of these groups and individuals rely, in great degree, on the *Protocols* to justify their anti-Semitism. Regrettably, only when these groups take dramatically violent action do the mainstream media inform us of their deeds and of any legal action taken against them: for instance, the trial of Timothy McVeigh; the Southern Poverty Law Center v. the Aryan Nation; the cases of Buford Furrow and Benjamin Smith; the truck-dragging lynching of James Byrd in Jasper, Texas; the homophobic-motivated murder of Matthew Shepard; and the massacre by students Klebold and Harris of other students at Columbine High School in Littleton, Colorado, on Hitler's birthday.

The use of the *Protocols* to justify their waves of rancor involves the panoply of right-wing extremist groups, and is applied to almost any issue or crisis situation:

> The militias have used Waco and Ruby Ridge as proof of long-standing conspiracy theories that the government will disarm all true patriots as a prelude to the United Nations taking over the United States as part of a New World Order orchestrated by international Jewish bankers. That belief goes back to the hoax text perpetrated on the world, the *Protocols of the Elders of Zion*. Although long ago proven to be totally false ... it is still held by the Patriot Movement as valid proof of its concerns.[9]

American Dissident Voices, for example, is a long-running radio program of the National Alliance, considered by many to be the most vociferous (and influential) of America's neo-Nazi anti-Semitic organizations, part of the self-proclaimed 'Patriot' movement. The text of each radio show is also presented on the Internet. The National Alliance leader, Dr William Pierce, who has been described as 'the white supremacist movement's undisputed master of propaganda'[10] and whose novel, *The Turner Diaries*, included a detailed prototype for the bombing that later occurred in Oklahoma City and allegedly had a strong influence on Timothy McVeigh's actions, has often used the *Protocols* as justification for his anti-Semitic tirades. In a broadcast on December 12 1998, entitled 'How It Fits Together', Pierce trumpeted the frequent allegations about Jews and the media:

> The Jewish media bosses know what they want. It is control — not of the media, but of us, of everything. They want to own us, and, to the extent they cannot own us, to destroy us. Unfortunately, I cannot play for you a secret recording of one of their summit meetings, where they discuss their goals and their strategy, àla *the Protocols of the Elders of Zion*. I can only offer you the historical record and common sense.[11]

In another Dissident Voice broadcast, on September 19, 1998, entitled 'A Confluence of Crises', Pierce stated that Russia's new prime minister, Yevgeny Primakov, was praised by the *The New York Times*, but that the *Times* did not reveal that Primakov, 'chosen by Berezosky and the other Jewish oligarchs,' was born Pinchas Finkelstein. 'Pinchas Finkelstein, prime minister of Russia,' Pierce stated. 'Amazing, isn't it? It's almost like something right out of the *Protocols of the Learned Elders of Zion*, this grasping, leering, insatiable greed of theirs.'[12]

> Henry Ford was one of the darlings of [American Dissident Voices] One Pierce broadcast, devoted to Ford and the Jews, stated: 'Henry Ford devoted years of his life and a substantial part of his fortune to awakening the American people to the enemies of our nation.'[13]

Notorious anti-Semite Gerald L. K. Smith alludes to the *Protocols* in an Internet blurb that praises Ford's publication and distribution of *The International Jew*. Smith states: 'When the report on *The International Jew* was originally published it opened each chapter with a text taken from 'the Protocols of the Learned Elders of Zion' ... He [Ford] said:

'Mr. Smith, my apology for publishing *The International Jew* was given great publicity, but I did not sign that apology.'[14]

The David Duke website uses the *Protocols* to promote Duke's book, *Jewish Supremacism: My Awakening on the Jewish Question*: 'Jewish authorities have tried to ban the book, fearing it will have a greater impact on the twenty-first-century world than the *Protocols of Zion* had on the twentieth century.'[15]

Some websites devote extensive space to introducing a new generation to the *Protocols*, and to proving their authenticity. Youth is a target audience of hate groups. National Alliance founder William Pierce has stated that many young people today are alienated and angry, and that 'my aim is to give them a target for their anger'.[16] For example, a site with a logo reading 'Be Wise as Serpents' and the headline 'The Protocols of the Elders of Zion' states the following:

> What are these 'Protocols of the Elders of Zion' which refuse to stay dead? In diplomacy, says the dictionary, protocols are 'a signed document containing a record of the points on which agreement has been reached by negotiating parties preliminary to a final treaty of 'compact'. These Protocols of Zion are a program for the enslavement of the world and the destruction of the Christian religion above all.
>
> Ever since their publication 'The Protocols of Zion' have been the most controversial writings in the world. Powerful elements in society have made them controversial so that few would be courageous enough to use them. We are all well aware that whoever uses the 'Protocols' as a legitimate reference is automatically labeled as a fool and an 'anti-Semite'...
>
> Many deceived Christian/Patriotic Researchers have stated that they are a product of the Bavarian Illuminati... Unfortunately, we will not be able to post all the evidence that we have – which is just as well – in spite of the voluminous evidence we could present that the 'Protocols' originated in secret Jewish meetings, we will probably not exclusively attempt to prove that here...[17]

A number of websites refer to or quote the *Protocols* as proof of a Jewish conspiracy whenever any event occurs that is similar to one or more allegations in the *Protocols*. One website, 'Jew Watch', asks those who log on to 'See How What the Protocols Said Has Been Done by the Jews Word-For-Word.'[18] For example, a review of a purportedly scholarly paper states the author's contention that 'the Protocols of Zion – the most tabooed book in the world – is an authentic document which contains a blueprint for Bolshevik Russia, and explains the terrible Debt crisis in the capitalist countries.'[19]

Passages from the *Protocols* referring to Jews seizing world power are frequently cited when any government appears to have one or more Jews in leadership positions, or a Jewish name is associated with the media. 'Stormfront', arguably the most sophisticated and effective of the extremist websites, promotes a book entitled *Truth At Last* with the following:

> The *Protocols of the Learned Elders of Zion*, was issued by Theodor Herzl to the Zionist Congress held in Basel, Switzerland in 1897. He outlines a plan for world power by gaining control of the media, politicians, governments, etc., to build the 'New World order'. Written 100 years ago, today we can see it's [sic] plans becoming a reality before our very own eyes.[20]

An example of such an application is a website entitled 'Know your Enemy', which, under the heading 'The Zion Protocols at Work – Who Runs the USA?', has published lists of 'Jews in the Clinton administration', 'The Jewish US–Ambassadors', 'Jewish Members of Congress', 'Jews in full control of US Media', and 'Jews or Jewish families who control the US financial markets'.[21]

Many websites in other countries around the world also use the *Protocols* to foment hate and violence against Jews. These include some Islamic websites, whose use of such rhetoric has coincided with the escalation of the Israeli–Palestinian conflict. Radio Islam, for example, corroborates some of the arguments stating that the *Protocols* are a forgery. 'Yet,' it states, 'if so long discredited, why have they become ... the most successful piece of propaganda in the twentieth century?' The site then attempts to demonstrate that the *Protocols*' prophecies have come true through Jewish and Gentile conspiracy. Quotes from the *Protocols* are used to fit today's issues and events.[22]

Shortly after the terrorist attacks of September 11 2001, a number of far-right websites began attributing the attacks to a Jewish plot motivated by the *Protocols of Zion*. One of the arguments presented to prove a Jewish conspiracy is akin to that used in the 1913 Bellis trial in czarist Russia: the World Trade Center attack was an instance of the Jews' devotion to ritual murder, as well as to monetary greed, as mandated by the *Protocols*.[23] A number of historical and literary references, including chapter 6 of the *International Jew* on the *Protocols of Zion*, are cited in order to justify the assertion that Jews were responsible for the Twin Towers attack. One site stated:

> How do you suppose that the Israelis knew about the WTC attack in NYC 2 hours ahead of time!? Only a few Jews died ... No wonder they were selling airline stocks short to make millions and millions. American Airlines and United Airlines stock were sold short ... several days before the 11th as were the stocks of corporations in the WTC. Millions were made by those Jews in the know.[24]

It is further unequivocally stated that the perpetrators of the September 11 attacks attended 'CIA arranged "flight schools" in Venice, Florida, which in turn could be linked to Jewish crime bosses linked to the Israeli Mossad.'[25]

While the radical right's exploitation of the *Protocols* can be found in their newsletters, newspapers, magazines, films, radio and public access television programs, the Internet has become their medium of choice. Allegations made in the *Protocols* may even be found in the lyrics on the widely distributed CD and tape recordings created by neo-Nazi rock bands. The Internet is a relatively inexpensive medium, it is anonymous in that its headquarters cannot be located by citizens in a given community who may object to the content, and it reaches, in real time, far more people than any other medium could. Don Black, the former Ku Klux Klan leader who operates the 'Stormfront' website and who has been credited with initiating the use of the Internet for the far right, has said: 'We are able to reach millions of people that we never had access to in the past. The Internet is becoming an alternative news medium for those who have an alternative point of view.'[26] William Pierce has commented:

> We've seen a huge growth in the use of the Internet by our people. The major media in this country are very biased against our political point of view. They present us with ridicule or in a very distorted way. The information highway is much more free of censorship. It's possible for a dedicated individual to get his message out to thousands and thousands of people.[27]

The leaders and backers of these extremist groups, the principal provocateurs, are rarely brought to trial. The wealthy and powerful go unpunished, and even unblemished. On the other hand, the foot soldiers, the Timothy McVeighs, who translate the hate rhetoric into violent action, are typically held accountable.

While there is little difference between the stated purpose and interpretation of the *Protocols* in the print materials distributed by the hate groups and on their websites, the websites provide greater flexibility as well as wider distribution. With few exceptions, materials in print are essentially analog or one-dimensional. That is, the story incorporating the allegations is usually a single piece, contained within the page or in one issue of the publication. Only occasionally is the story part of a series of articles on the same subject, or incorporates the narrative of other works. Essentially, the recipient receives the material passively; that is, she or he is rarely able to access additional material on the subject instantaneously. The Internet, however, is interactive. It not only provides instant links, but encourages the individual to access them. People who log on to any given hate site may not be looking for material about the *Protocols*, and may even be unfamiliar with them. Icons on numerous sites linking to the *Protocols* provide an introduction for many, and for others an ideological reinforcement.

In addition, the lag time between the production and reception of printed materials frequently precludes the inclusion of events that might enhance the allegations in print. Websites can – as in the instance of September 11, 2001 – be changed and re-imaged immediately to take advantage of new events that can be alleged to have been motivated by the *Protocols*. The Internet has facilitated the resurrection of the *Protocols*, giving the rumors and the distortions of truth more breadth and depth in cyberspace than they ever had in traditional communication modes, following the general acceptance of their falsity.

The contemporary use of the *Protocols* to justify bigotry is directly analogous to what was happening a century, three-quarters of a century and – in the case of the calculated anti-Semitism of the US government and State Department in denying asylum and immigration to Jews trying to escape the Nazi Holocaust – little more than a half-century ago. The past is important, however, only to the extent to which we apply its lessons today.

Undoubtedly, the legacy of the *Protocols* is still with us. The anti-Semitism that destroyed six million Jews in World War II, and countless others before and since, is a growing danger in the USA. I hope it will be our individual and mutual commitment to do more than study and talk about it, but to take action to counter the inroads made by these hate groups and their plans for a Holocaust in America. Let us give the public the truth with our own Internet sites, let us write letters to the editor, let us call in to talk shows when we hear hate spewing from extremists, let us consciously become active in our own communities to achieve workable multicultural societies, let us participate in local government and politics in ways that will prevent these hate groups from gaining footholds on our school boards and city councils, as they have done in so many places. Only through such individual and mutually dedicated action will we be able to prevent the new planned horrors generated by the legacy of the *Protocols of the Learned Elders of Zion*.

NOTES

1. Stephen Bronner, *A Rumor About the Jews: Anti-Semitism, Conspiracy, and the 'Protocols of Zion'*. (New York: St Martin's Press, 2000, p. 107.
2. 'The Assailants of the Jew', editorial, *New York Times*, 1 December 1 1920, p. 19.
3. Norman Cohn, *Warrant for Genocide*. (London: Serif Publishers, 1996).
4. Neil Baldwin, *Henry Ford and the Jews* (New York: Public Affairs Press, 2001), p. 173.
5. Ibid., p. 185.
6. Michael Dobbs, 'Ford and GM Scrutinized for Alleged Nazi Collaboration', *Washington Post*, November 30 1998,
7. Binjamin Segal, and Richard Levy (trans. and ed.), *A Lie and a Libel: the History of the Protocols of the Elders of Zion* (Lincoln: University of Nebraska Press, 1995), p. 26.
8. Bronner, *Rumour About the Jews*, p. 5.
9. Robert Hilliard, and Michael Keith, *Waves of Rancor: Tuning in the Radical Right* (Armonk, NY: M.E. Sharpe, 1999), p. 187.
10. Ibid., p. 166.
11. www.natvan.com/pub/98/121298.txt. Site last consulted December 15 2001.
12. www.natvan.com/pub/98/091998.txt. Site last consulted December15 2001.
13. Hilliard and Keith, *Waves of Rancor*, pp. 174-5.
14. www.jrbooksonline.com/intro_by_gerald_smith.htm. Site last consulted 26 January 2002
15. www.duke.org/supremacism/. Site last consulted January 26 2002.
16. David Segal, 'Rage against the minorities,' *Boston Globe*, January 20 2000.
17. www.iahushua.com/BeWise/protocol.html. Site last consulted January 26 2002.
18. www.jewwatch.com/jew-references-*Protocols*-folder.html. Site last consulted January 26 2002.
19. users.cyberone.com.au/myers/hiding.html. Site last consulted January 26 2002. This statement was no longer posted in a December 2005 check of this site.
20. www.stormfront.org/wpww/library/archives/text_files-sorted/books/learned-elders.htm. Site last consulted January 26 2002.
21. home.att.net/—azawawi/know_your_enemy.htm accessed through home.att.net on January 26 2002..
22. www.abbc.com/islam/english/toread/prvisit.htm. accessed through www.intellecy.com on January 26 2002.

23. Ibid.
24. www.intellex.com/—rigs/page1/wtc/wtc.htm. Site last consulted January 26 2002..
25. Ibid.
26. Hilliard and Keith, *Waves of Rancor*, p. 28.
27. Ibid., p. 115.

4

The Protocols of the Elders of Zion: Group Defamation Trials in Civil Courts and in the 'Court' of Public Opinion

FREDERICK M. LAWRENCE

Our task is to discuss ways in which assertions of truth and falsity can be made in the academy and in our public civic institutions. Our particular task is to consider these complex questions in the context of the *Protocols of the Elders of Zion*.[1]

In the previous chapter, Robert Hilliard ended with a clarion call not to overlook the risks with which we still live, and he certainly is right. It is a time for vigilance, perhaps not overkill, but certainly vigilance. But permit me, by way of transition, to begin with an uplifting story. It concerns one of the most powerful moments in the history of the treatment of and reaction to American anti-Semitism. The climactic event of the story went by very quietly; you might easily have missed it. Its lead-up, however, did not pass quietly at all. The story begins with a notorious speech in 1994 by Khalid Abdul Mohammad, one of the main leaders of the Nation of Islam, a man who repeated all of the vulgarities that have been spewed about Judaism with which we have all become too familiar – that it is a 'gutter religion', – and about Jewish behavior and Jewish activities within the United States and in the international community. The uplifting and remarkable moment was the response of the Anti-Defamation League (ADL). A full-page advertisement was taken in the *New York Times* that merely repeated the speech, verbatim. At the bottom of the page was printed '[t]he Anti-Defamation League – founded in 1913, is the world's leading organization fighting anti-Semitism through programs and services that counteract hatred, prejudice and bigotry.'[2] This was truly a breathtaking moment. The ADL acted on the assumption that no rebuttal of Abdul Mohammad's statements was necessary, and that the mere exposing of the falsehood would be sufficient to assert the truth.

When Stephen Bronner talks about the *Protocols* having been 'proved to be a forgery,' he says, 'it is indisputable'.[3] But proven to whom? Proven how? That is the critical concern of this chapter. Bronner proves it to *me* in his book.[4] But to whom generally does one prove this assertion, and by what measure may we judge the proof to be satisfactory, let alone indisputable? Who wants to listen? And how do we go about proving it? All of these questions, for the purposes of this volume, become the question of how best to respond to the *Protocols*. The specific context I will address is the sustained affirmation and assertion of the *Protocols*, through the 1920s, in a series of articles in Henry Ford's newspaper, the *Dearborn Independent*.[5] How do we prove that the arguments contained in the *Protocols* are wrong? Do we merely repeat them, as the ADL did? Do we rebut the arguments or combat them? In short, how does one prove them to be false?

I would like to sketch out the three formal means in which responses to the *Protocols* might have been made, and how truth and falsity might have been weighed. I will consider the benefits and risks of each, the cost of each, and then suggest a different way in which it might have played out. Two modes of response involve actual litigation: individual libel and group libel, but I will start with another one, that of Congressional investigation.

The option of seeking a Congressional investigation began during the very time in which the *Dearborn Independent* continued to produce articles based on the falsehoods of the *Protocols*. The American-Jewish Committee and the ADL, two of the leading American Jewish organizations of the time,[6] considered launching efforts to bring about a Congressional investigation of the *Independent* and of Ford.[7] Congressional investigations have certain advantages over litigation. For example, they allow significantly looser limits on the admissibility of evidence than the formal admissibility of evidence required in a court trial. The issues for a Congressional investigation may be broad and, relative to the courtroom, there are few limitations on what may be considered 'relevant', a word that lawyers live with on a daily basis, certainly in the courtroom. 'Relevance' to a Congressional Committee is generally as broad as the committee wishes it to be.

There is, however, also an underside to this advantage. The broad interpretation of relevance and admissibility in a Congressional investigation affects not only the party seeking the investigation and hoping to introduce evidence to Congress, but every other aspect of the investigation as well. If the party seeking the investigation is not bound by rules of evidence, neither is anyone else. We live in a time when no one needs to be persuaded of the risks of Congressional investigations. The images that come to mind might, for instance, include the Whitewater investigation that culminated in the impeachment of President Clinton. However, were we living some 50 years ago, you might still be nodding in agreement, but would likely be thinking of Senator Joseph McCarthy, or perhaps the investigations and hearings held by the House Un-American Activities Committee. This is not a new problem: Congressional investigations consider a plethora of information from which it is difficult to discern the pertinent facts. It was largely for this reason that Louis Marshall of the American Jewish Committee was opposed to pursuing the strategy of seeking Congressional investigations. He feared that the record would be filled with the stuff and nonsense of his enemies, or, as he put it, such an investigation 'would enable our enemies to shovel into the record all kinds of stupid and inane charges'.[8]

In a sense, the process of a politicized search for – and we cannot avoid the use of quotation marks here – 'truth', shows us that in an ironic, almost absurd way, the search for the truth represented by a Congressional investigation is overtly postmodern. There is an abandonment of any sense of objective truth, and in its place an assertion of normative positions advanced by each side. For instance, any of us who has had the experience of testifying before Congress knows that witnesses are asked by one side or the other to testify. There is something flattering, but also alarming, about being called by either the committee chair, or the ranking minority member of the committee, and being told that 'you're my witness'. Once, when I received such a call, I remember thinking that I was supposed simply to be *a* witness. But it was made clear to me that I was *someone's* witness and that this was a major reason why I was called to testify in the first place. There is a role for Congressional investigations, and there are ways in which they may even work quite well. But as a search for the 'truth', Congressional investigations are perhaps a very dangerous approach, and ultimately not one that the American-Jewish community was interested in pursuing during the 1920s as a response to Henry Ford and the *Dearborn Independent*.

What about litigation, and specifically, libel suits? The individual libel suit is the one that is best known to us. That is, the standard defamation or slander case brought by an individual asserting that he or she has had a reputation slandered and harmed by the defendant. Group libel, on behalf of an entire group or ethnic community, asserts that the group collectively has been attacked and harmed in some sense. The *Dearborn Independent* accused Aaron Sapiro, a San Francisco attorney, and certain other Jews of using farm cooperatives to seize control of American agriculture (see also Hilliard, Chapter 3).[9] Sapiro brought allegations against the *Dearborn Independent* for slander both on his own behalf individually and on behalf of the Jewish community collectively, or, as he described it, 'myself and my race'.[10] All of the group allegations ultimately were dismissed by the trial judge, leaving only the individual claims involving Sapiro himself.[11]

The dismissal of the group claims in Sapiro's case against the *Independent* is highly relevant for our inquiry. The Sapiro defamation case was notorious in its time. Each age has had its great trials that have become the focus of the general public. Some of these, such as the Lindbergh baby kidnapping trial or the Sacco and Vanzetti trial, remain well known. Others, such as Aaron Sapiro's defamation case, are all but lost to us now. The Sapiro defamation case preoccupied the Jewish community, and even beyond it. At the time, many in the general public followed the case to see what would happen in court.[12] Nevertheless, once the group aspects are taken out, what we are left with is a libel claim by one individual. Then, only evidence that is directly and specifically relevant to that individual charge is admissible in court. The very courtroom itself seems smaller as soon as we say that. The entire context becomes smaller. Inevitably, the case becomes de-contextualized. It is about Aaron Sapiro's individual libel claim. This narrowing of the issues cannot help but lose a large element of the life-blood of the case, which was, after all, about the anti-Semitic calumny that had underpinned the entire charge.

Also inevitably, the case concludes at best with a hollow victory. The greatest victory that Aaron Sapiro could win was a verdict based on a finding that he had not used farm cooperatives illegally to try to seize control of American agriculture. The blood libel case discussed in chapters 2 and 3 is analogous. In the blood libel case, an acquittal is actually a conviction; a win is a kind of loss. In a much more trivial way, one is reminded of the old joke of the 'defender' who tells his friend that 'someone said you weren't fit to sleep with the pigs, and I defended you by saying that "You are too fit to sleep with the pigs."' Or perhaps better, one is reminded of the classic leading question asking a man when had he 'stopped beating his wife'. The general leading question contains the implication of proof as to the general crime; the specific defense cannot completely remove the general taint. The acquittal in the blood libel trial runs the risk of being an acquittal only of the individual charge that the accused himself did not engage in the behavior asserted in the libel. What the acquittal actually means is that the blood libel generally is accurate, but inapplicable in this particular case. Sapiro's victory would mean that he personally did not try to seize control of American agriculture, but this would leave untouched – or worse, implicitly validate – the allegation that American Jews, albeit American Jews other than Aaron Sapiro, were engaged in such behavior. The individual acquittal becomes the group conviction.

In the individual libel case, it becomes impossible to get at the heart of the fundamental truth claims. Precisely because the truth claims and the falsity claims that are advanced and evaluated in the courtroom are necessarily limited to the individual case, they are de-contextualized. The individual defamation suit is not without its place or purpose. Obviously, it plays an important role in restoring the individual victim's reputation. But ultimately, the individual libel suit cannot be a way of testing the truth and falsity of the group claims, or of what I have called the fundamental truth claims. Sapiro's reputation may be restored by the verdict of an individual libel suit, but the truth and falsity of the *Protocols* cannot be evaluated in this manner.

Group defamation suits might appear to provide a context for weighing the truth or falsity of claims such as those contained in the *Protocols*. But the very concept of group libel raises serious issues of free expression, concerns that were true at the time of the *Dearborn Independent* controversy,[13] and have only become more so since then because of the evolution of free speech doctrine.[14]

A full evaluation of group libel doctrine and its constitutional ramifications cannot be adequately explored here. For now, however, let me make the following cautionary comments about group libel. Among its core values, free expression doctrine protects the right to have, hold and express our personal opinions and beliefs.[15] Either in a procedural context or in a broader constitutional context, issues of truth and falsehood cannot help but conflate with issues of opinion and belief, and thus implicate core free expression values. As a procedural matter, the question in a defamation suit, at least in a suit involving a public figure, is not so much whether what the defendant said was true or false, but whether the defendant knew it was false or acted with reckless disregard for the truth.[16] All of this focuses, and must focus, on the mind of the actor. Necessarily, this takes us away from truth and falsehood *per se* and to issues of opinion and belief.

If we shift from the narrow procedural questions concerning the specific elements that must be proven, to a more constitutional, theoretical context, questions of group libel and opinions concerning ethnic groups and religious groups cannot help but run squarely into questions of free expression. I am reminded of Robert Hughes's essay concerning the controversial exhibition of photographs by Robert Mapplethorpe in the early 1990s.[17] Sometimes lawyers need non-lawyers to call our attention to profound truths concerning the legal system. Hughes observed that the questions concerning the exhibition of Mapplethorpe's photographs had become largely a discussion about whether or not the exhibiting of this work was constitutionally protected. The debate, therefore, is centered around whether, as a matter of constitutional right, a museum may exhibit this work, or whether a city may, as Cincinnati, Ohio did, shut such an exhibition down.[18] When, however, we focus on these questions of constitutional limits of expression and municipal authority to regulate expression, we preclude asking a more important question: as a matter of art criticism and aesthetics, not of constitutional doctrine and theory, is this art any good? Some of it may be terrific, some of it may be okay, and one might argue, given the opportunity, that some of it is terrible. But we cannot even have that discussion if we remain preoccupied solely with the constitutional questions. When we are caught up in such questions, as we must be about the right to say certain things and to express certain opinions, we lose the context in which to have the vital discussion of whether the assertion under consideration is any good as history, or any good as philosophy, or good as art, or good as literature. What is the context in which Stephen Bronner gets to say, 'it's indisputable that the *Protocols* is wrong?' Probably not in a group libel case.

The case against Henry Ford and the *Dearborn Independent* was tried, in a sense, before the 'court of public opinion', a terribly hackneyed expression, but, I think, very helpful here. When we think about the 'court' of public opinion, it permits us to conceive of it as another kind of quasi-judicial proceeding. Although I do not wish to overuse the metaphor, I think it will help us to understand the context of broad-based public debate as an example of another kind of forum, or 'court', in which a form of litigation may occur.

How is a case litigated in the court of public opinion? The promulgation of the *Protocols* in the *Dearborn Independent* is illustrative. The case against Ford and the *Independent* was litigated, first and foremost, by a counter-leaflet issued by the American-Jewish community called 'The Protocols, Bolshevism and the Jews', and addressed to the American public. This remarkable leaflet was essentially a legal brief addressed to the court of public opinion. The American-Jewish community also organized a boycott of Ford, as well as a petition of prominent Americans, including Presidents Taft and Wilson, that was highly critical of Ford.[19] The sustained effort had a negative impact on Ford economically and, of perhaps even greater significance to him, also on his own political ambitions. The association of the *Independent* with the *Protocols* became an embarrassment from which Ford had to disassociate himself.[20]

We should contrast the success of this 'litigation' in the court of American public opinion with the European context of the same time. In Europe of the 1920s, the *Protocols* continued to be published, and to have an extraordinary and tragic impact.[21] Why is it that the court of public opinion worked in the 1920s in America in a way that it did not in Germany? For that matter, why did the court of public opinion to which the Anti-Defamation League presented its response to Khalid Abdul Mohammad in the United States in the 1990s work differently from that of either the United States or Europe in the 1920s? I have two observations, or rather, two additional questions we should ask about the court of public opinion. The first is whether we are talking about a matter of broad-based group issues that will capture public attention. If not, we would not expect the court of public opinion to give us any satisfaction as a way of thinking about truth or falsity of claims or issues; in such instances, individual libel cases may be the only answer. It will give us partial answers, but perhaps those are the only answers we can obtain, however imperfect and de-contextualized they may be. If, however, we have an issue that will focus public attention, then perhaps we can think about an address to the general public and to a national community, and consider bringing the case to the court of public opinion.

The second question is much more amorphous, but I dare say much more important as well. It concerns the normative context of the society in which the argument is made. As my late teacher, Robert Cover, wrote, 'We inhabit a *nomos*',[22] an unavoidably normative social context. It is into this *nomos* that the argument must be placed, and within the context of this *nomos* that the debate must be developed. In the 1920s in

America, the court of public opinion could be turned to, but it required a counter-leaflet, a kind of direct argument. In the court of public opinion in the America of the 1990s, the ADL operated under the assumption that the defamatory allegations themselves were sufficient to make a rebuttal. Repeating the falsehood was sufficient to assert the truth.

Let me end with the story of a correspondence between Mahatma Gandhi and Martin Buber during the 1930s. Gandhi, who was not sympathetic to Zionism as a program, argued that the proper response to rising Nazism was passive resistance.[23] Buber reminded Gandhi, in essence, that whereas Gandhi was dealing with the British, Buber was dealing with Nazis.[24] Non-violent resistance against the British in India was an entirely different proposition from non-violent resistance against Nazis in central and eastern Europe, and ultimately in western Europe. When you are dealing with Nazis, you cannot act as if you are dealing with the British. When you are dealing with the British, it is not the same as dealing with Americans. And Americans in the 1920s talking about Jews is not the same as Americans in the 1920s talking about Blacks, which is not the same as Americans in the 1990s talking about Jews, which is not the same as Americans talking about Blacks in the 1990s, either.

To understand the nature of a particular court of public opinion, to grasp its rules and to contemplate a litigation strategy before it, requires that we understand the social context from which that court arises. Such an inquiry will help us in turn to understand the extent of that court's 'jurisdiction', that is, the type of issues that may be brought before the court, and indeed whether, in a particular time or place, the court exists at all. Only when there is a less prejudicial social climate can the kind of truth–falsity discussions we are considering have any hope of being adjudicated in the court of public opinion, that is, adjudicated in a way that might provide the parties and the society with a full and meaningful 'remedy'.

NOTES

1. Debra Kaufman's idea at the international conference was to provide a forum in which each of the participants, from different perspectives and different methodologies, would spark one another and affect one another's analyses. It proved very effective..
2. The advertisement appeared in the *New York Times* on 14 January 1994, p. 27.
3. Stephen E. Bronner, see Chapter 2.
4. Stephen E. Bronner, *A Rumor About the Jews: Reflections on Anti-Semitism and the Protocols of the Learned Elders of Zion*, (New York: St Martin's Press, 2000).
5. See Neil Baldwin, *Henry Ford and the Jews* (New York: St Martin's Press 2001), pp. 209–10; Leonard Dinnerstein, *Anti-Semitism in America* (New York: St Martin's Press, 1994), pp. 81-2; Albert Lee, *Henry Ford and the Jews* (New York: Stein Day, 1980), pp. 68–72; Evan P. Schultz, Group Rights, American Jews, and the Failure of Group Libel Laws, 1913-1952, *Brooklyn Law Review* (2000), Vol. 66, No. 71, pp. 100–11.

6. See Jacob Rader Marcus, *The American Jew: 1585-1990, A History* (Brooklyn, NY: Carlson, 1995), p. 305; Deborah Dash Moore, *B'Nai B'rith and the Challenge of Ethnic Leadership* (Albany, NY: State University of New York Press, 1981), pp 102–16); Howard M. Sachar, *A History of the Jews in America* (New York: Random House, 1993), pp. 307-8 1993).
7. *Letter from Louis Marshall to Rabbi Isaac Landsman* (Dec. 24, 1920), in Charles Reznikoff (ed.), *Louis Marshall: Champion of Liberty* (Philadelphia, PA: Jewish Publication Society, 1957), p. 350, n.; Schultz, 'Group Rights', pp. 102–03, n.5.
8. *Letter from Louis Marshall to Adolf Kraus* (6 Apr 1921), in Reznikoff, *Louis Marshall: Champions of Liberty*, 350 n.7, quoted in Schultz, 'Group Rights', p. 103.
9. Baldwin, *Henry Ford and the Jews*, at pp. 209–11; Lee, *Henry Ford and the Jews*, pp. 68–71; Schultz, *Group Rights*, pp. 109-10.
10. Sachar, *History of the Jews*, p. 317.
11. Baldwin, *Henry Ford and the Jews*, p. 219; Schultz, 'Group Rights', p. 10.
12. The *New York Times* (*NYT*), for example, devoted extensive coverage to the Sapiro defamation case during the trial. Daily coverage of the trial often made the front page. See for example, 'All Ready to Start Ford-Sapiro Trial,' *NYT*, 14 March 1927, p. 1; 'Sapiro Fights Hard to Put Henry Ford on Witness Stand,' *NYT*, 15 March 1927, p. 1; Ford will Specify A 'Different Band' as Sapiro's Aides, *NYT*, 21 March 1927, p. 1; Mistrial Sought by Ford's Counsel, *NYT*, 28 March 1927, at 1; Ford Gets Mistrial in $1,000,000 Suit; Sapiro to Fight It, *NYTs*, 22 April 1927, p. 1; Ford and Sapiro Settle Libel Suit, *NYT*, 16 July 1927, p. 1.
13. Schultz, 'Group Rights', pp. 104–08.
14. The Supreme Court upheld a group libel statute in *Beauharnais* v. *Illinois*, 343 U.S. 250, 258-63 (1952): 'we are precluded from saying that speech concededly punishable when immediately directed at individuals cannot be outlawed if directed at groups with whose position and esteem in society the affiliated individual may be inextricably involved.' Nevertheless, 'it has become a commonplace of constitutional law discussions that the case is no longer good law.' Lee Bollinger, 'Rethinking Group Libel,' in (Monroe H. Freedman and Eric M. Freedman, (eds) *Group Defamation and Freedom of Speech*, (Westport, CT: Greenwood Press, 1995), p. 243. *Beauharnais* was undercut, for example, by *Brandenburg* v. *Ohio* 395 U.S. 444, 447 (1969): 'constitutional guarantees of free speech and free press do not permit a State to forbid or proscribe advocacy of the use of force or of law violation except where such advocacy is directed to inciting or producing imminent lawless action and is likely to incite or produce such action.' See *R.A.V.* v. *City of St Paul*, 505 U.S. 377, 382-392 (1992) (continuing vitality of *Beauharnais* has been questioned given *New York Times* v. *Sullivan* requirement of actual malice, but has not been explicitly overruled). See, also Eric Freedman 'A Lot More Comes Into Focus When You Remove the Lens Cap: Why Proliferating New Communications Technologies Make It Particularly Urgent for the Supreme Court to Abandon Its Inside-Out Approach to Freedom of Speech and Bring Obscenity, Fighting Words, and Group Libel Within the First Amendment,' *Iowa Law Review*, 81 (1996) pp. 883, 950-52; William B. Fisch, 'Hate Speech in the Constitutional Law of the United States', *American Journal of Comparative Law*, pp. 463, 478-82 (Fall 2002).
15. See Thomas I. Emerson, *The System of Freedom of Expression* (New York: Vintage Books, 1970), p.3; *Palko* v. *Connecticut*, 302 U.S. (1937), p. 319: 'freedom of thought and speech ... is the matrix, the indispensable condition, of nearly ever other form of freedom.' See also for example, Frederick Schauer, *Free Speech: A Philosophical Enquiry* (1984); Steven Shiffrin, *The First Amendment, Democracy, and Romance* (1990).
16. See *New York Times Co.* v. *Sullivan*, 376 U.S. 254 (1964); Rodney Smolla, *Law of Defamation* §§3:3 (2nd. ed., 1999). The vast majority of states require less than knowledge or reckless disregard of falsity in defamation cases filed by *private* citizens. Nevertheless, negligence is a required minimum in all defamation cases. *Gertz* v. *Robert Welch, Inc.*, 418 U.S. 323 (1974). See generally, Smolla, *Law of Defamation* §§3:3–3:4, 3:30.
17. Robert Hughes, 'Art, Morals, and Politics',' *New York Review of Books*, 23 April 1992, pp. 21-7.
18. Eric Harrison, 'Mapplethorpe Display Brings Smut Charges', *LA Times*, 8 April 1990, p. A1; Isabel Wilkerson, 'Cincinnati Gallery Indicted In Mapplethorpe Furor', *NYT*, 8 April 1990, § 1, p. 1; Isabel Wilkerson, 'Cincinnati Jury Acquits Museum In Mapplethorpe Obscenity Case', *NYT*, 6 October 1990, § 1, p. 1.
19. Reznikoff, *Louis Marshall: VChampion of Liberty*, p. 354. Other notable signatories included Charles A. Beard, William Jennings Bryan, Robert Frost, Paul D. Cravath, W. H. B. Du Bois,

Clarence Darrow and the presidents of Princeton, Brown and Columbia Universities, John Grier Hibben, W. H. P. Faunce and Nicholas Murray Butler, respectively.
20. Baldwin, *Henry Ford and the Jews*, pp. 224, 235-6; Schultz, 'Group Rights', pp. 102, 108.
21. Norman Cohn, *Warrant for Genocide: The Myth of the Jewish World Conspiracy and the Protocols of the Elders of Zion* (Harmansworth: Penguin, 1970), pp. 181-3; Nora Levin, *The Holocaust: The Destruction of European Jewry 1933-1945* (New York: Schocker Books, 1973), pp. 18-19, 39; Benjamin W. Segel, *A Lie and Libel: The History of the Protocols of the Elders of Zion* (trans.and ed. Richard S. Levy 1995), pp. 31–32..
22. Robert M. Cover, 'The Supreme Court, 1982 Term – Foreword: Nomos and Narrative', 97 *Harvard Law Review*, 4 (1983): 'We inhabit a *nomos* – a normative universe. We constantly create and maintain a world of right and wrong, of lawful and unlawful, of valid and void ... In this normative world, law and narrative are inseparably related. Every prescription is insistent in its demand to be located in discourse – to be supplied with history and destiny, beginning and end, explanation and purpose. And every narrative is insistent in its demand for its prescriptive point, its moral.'
23. The statement was published on 26 November 1938 in the weekly, *Harijan*. See Martin Buber, *The Letters of Martin Buber: A Life of Dialogue*, (eds Nahum N. Glatzer and Paul Mendes-Flohr,trans. Richard Winston *et al*, 1991), p. 476.
24. Ibid., pp. 476-86: 'Now, do you know or do you not know, Mahatma, what a concentration camp is like and what goes on there ... Indians were despised and despicably treated in South Africa. But they were not deprived of rights, they were not outlawed, they were not hostages to a hoped-for change in the behavior of foreign powers ... Of what significance is it to point to a certain something in common when such differences are overlooked?'

5

The Persistence of Falsehood and the Protocols of the Elders of Zion

MARTHA MINOW[1]

Reading about the history of the *Protocols of the Elders of Zion*, I am most struck by the persistence of rumor and falsehood. Inspite of careful historical, journalistic and legal inquiry conducted over many decades, the document and its patent lies continue to circulate and to gain wide readership. Granted, readers of any source can and should remain skeptical, even when the source claims to refute the veracity of another document. Journalists, historians and lawyers can manipulate listeners with the appearance of truth-telling, without actually uncovering the truth. In the case of the *Protocols*, however, journalists, historians and lawyers have definitively refuted both its contents and alleged provenance. Why, then, do the document and its falsehood persist?

The growing attention to the history of rumor may offer us some guidance.[2] So too may studies of prejudice and its resistance to refutation.[3] Rumors and falsehoods circulate and resist eradication when they meet a need: a need for scapegoats, a need for demarcating 'we' and 'they', a need for attributing evil. At times, a falsehood may endure because it echoes other cultural or religious sources, even though similarly unsubstantiated. The mere resonance and reverberation lends credibility. Unscrupulous leaders, with hateful messages amplified through broadcasting and cyberspace, trigger memories of childhood stories or supply psychologically satisfying outlets for current frustrations. A falsehood can persist when it is flexible, able to be recast to avoid direct refutation or reinvented to serve different purposes. All of these features characterize the *Protocols of the Elders of Zion*.

Widely recognized now as a forgery and tissue of lies, the *Protocols* proclaim a global conspiracy of Zionist Jews who plot to take over the world.[4] Sergei Nilus included the text first in a 1905 publication and then in an expanded form in 1917.[5] As early as 1921, observers concluded that the *Protocols* were a distorted and plagiarized version of a French dialogue by satirist Maurice Joly, whose own work never mentioned Jews and who aimed its critique at authoritarianism.[6] A German postal clerk and secret police spy named Hermann Goedsche, under the pseudonym Sir John Retcliffe, lifted sections of Joly's political satire when he recast the material as a tale of Jewish conspiracy. In turn, this text appeared in a Russian translation; Russian agents edited and distributed another version, now called *The Protocols of the Elders of Zion*, during the Dreyfus Affair in Paris. A manuscript brought to Russia in 1895 received private publication in 1897 and public distribution in 1905, when reactionary organizations sought to blame the 1905 Revolution on the Jews. Historians found copies of the text in the collection of the czar, along with evidence that he knew it to be a forgery.[7] *The Protocols of the Elders of Zion* is thus a forged and revamped version of a fiction.

The United States Congress, journalists and historians have concluded that the *Protocols* lack any truth.[8] Nonetheless, the document continues to be published and widely distributed, generating astronomical sales.[9] Historian Henri Rollin described the *Protocols* as the most widely distributed book in the world other than the Bible.[10] During their rise to power in Germany, the Nazis used the *Protocols*, as have neo-fascist and anti-Semitic groups, since the Second World War. The document is most widely distributed today in Arab countries, including versions published by government presses in Egypt in the 1960s and 1970s, by Radio Islam in the 1980s, and through the Internet into the twenty-first century.[11]

The *Protocols* found a receptive audience because their content resonated with longstanding European traditions scapegoating Jews, who were depicted as dangerous and conniving. These stories served the purposes of unscrupulous leaders and pandered to the political, religious and economic needs of non-Jewish masses. The Jews served as ready and repeated targets of blame for a variety of social misfortunes. Not surprising, the document emerged in close to its current form at the time of the Dreyfus Affair, an event epitomizing the early twentieth-century escalation of anti-Semitic beliefs in military, legal and political settings. In the repeated trials of Alfred Dreyfus unfounded charges stuck for years, because military and social desires elevated scapegoating over finding the truth. Henry Ford, the automobile magnate, published a version of the *Protocols* in his anti-Semitic newspaper the *Dearborn Independent*, in the 1920s. Adolf Hitler cited and endorsed the *Protocols* in his autobiography, *Mein Kampf*.[12]

Legal challenges, seeking to halt circulation and to debunk the *Protocols*, have generated trials in Switzerland, South Africa, the United States and Russia.[13] The two most prominent cases, however, failed to provide definitive refutation. Hermann Bernstein, who wrote a book in 1921 exposing the *Protocols* as a forgery, brought a libel action against Henry Ford after he had circulated the *Protocols* first in the *Dearborn Independent*, and then in a book, *The International Jew: The World's Foremost Problem*. Approximately 500,000 copies of the book circulated in the United States, with translations in German, Russian, Spanish and ultimately 15 more languages. Before World War II, the Nazis used an abridged version of the book as a key propaganda piece.[14] Ford initially defended the libel suit, but ultimately, in 1927, as part of a negotiated settlement, he wrote a letter of apology that indicated he was unaware that the *Protocols* were forged, that he had been too busy to read the newspaper, and that it would cease printing materials pertaining to Jews.[15] Ford closed the newspaper, but later objected that his signature on the letter of apology was forged—and also later blamed World War II on Jewish bankers.[16] He did not, and could not, recall all the copies circulating in the world.[17]

The second major legal challenge to the *Protocols of the Elders of Zion* occurred in 1933, when institutional representatives of Jews in Switzerland brought a suit charging that Theodor Fischer of the Swiss National Socialists and Silvio Schnell of the National Front of Switzerland had violated the Berne law against distributing improper literature by circulating the document.[18] Relying on historians and other experts, the plaintiffs mounted evidence that the *Protocols* were a forgery, and also argued that circulation of the document violated the law.[19] Vladimir Burtsev, a key witness who had edited a Russian paper and then a Paris Russian paper, later wrote a book based on his testimony. At the trial, he indicated that he had been arrested by the Bolsheviks after the overthrow of the Provisional government, and shared a cell with a man named S. P. Beletskii, who had been Director of Police and then the Assistant Minister of Internal Affairs from 1910 to 1919. Burtsev asked this former official whether the government intended to offer the *Protocols* during the ritual murder trial in 1913 of Mendel Beilis, a

Russian Jew accused of killing a young Christian boy in order to extract blood for a supposedly religious ritual. Beletskii acknowledged that this strategy had been considered, but had been cast aside because government officials were aware that the *Protocols* were widely known to be a forgery, and therefore did not want their introduction at trial to spoil the prosecution of Beilis.[20]

At the Berne trial, held in a city police court, the defendants' did not claim that the *Protocols* were authentic or true, but simply argued that the publication fell outside the scope of the law prohibiting improper literature.[21] The court rejected this defense and produced a seemingly decisive judgment for the plaintiffs: it found the *Protocols* to be a plagiary and declared their contents inauthentic, harmful and ridiculous nonsense.[22] It was short-lived victory, however. On appeal, the defendants successfully gained a reversal on the technical grounds that the *Protocols* were not improper in the sense intended by the Berne law, because they were not salacious.[23] The appellate court did describe the defendants preface to the *Protocols* as entirely perfidious and an unwarranted insult against one part of the Swiss people, yet it also indicated that formal legal denunciation was unnecessary because the cool judgment of the Swiss people would prevail.[24] In light of the appellate decision, however, the Swiss courts provided no legal protection against the lies of the *Protocols*.

More recently, courts have been willing to repudiate the *Protocols of the Elders of Zion*. In 1990 a Swedish court forbade the broadcast of the *Protocols* by a radio station called Radio Islam, operated by Ahmed Rami; Rami was found guilty of the crime of incitement, and the conviction was upheld on appeal.[25] After serving his sentence, Rami re-established Radio Islam as an Internet site, maintained on a server in the United States.[26] In 1993, a Russian court pronounced the *Protocols of the Elders of Zion* an anti-Semitic forgery.[27] The court relied in part on testimony by a three-member panel of Russian academic experts, agreed to by both sides on the sole stipulation that none of them was Jewish.

As evidenced by cases that involved the *Protocols*, litigation has strengths and limitations in struggles to resolve debates over truth. The strengths include cross-examination, to test the credibility of witnesses and content of testimony; powers of subpoena and discovery to unearth material even over the objection of those who possess it; and adversarial argument to expose the weaknesses of assertions, polemical claims and narratives lacking factual foundation. Judicial process also can turn to procedural rules, such as burden of proof, to help resolve questions. Adversarial argument is, however, one of the limitations of the judicial approach, because it animates and can keep alive the counter-view, even after an apparent verdict or judgment against it. Additional limitations of litigation are even more profound. Courts force complex situations into narrow questions – such as, are the *Protocols of the Elders of Zion* 'improper literature', yes or no? Litigation takes a long time. It is expensive, and is affected by the skill of the advocates and the biases of the judges. The credibility of the experts readily becomes a potential ground for disagreement. In some courts, individuals may be treated as experts simply because they have gained notoriety through numerous publications; others who are widely respected within their own professions may appear uncertain or ineffective in the very different context of adversarial litigation. While skilled attorneys can expose the lack of factual foundation for a seemingly compelling narrative, courts themselves ultimately depend upon persuasive narratives. Typically, these are stories crafted by the litigants' counsel. These narratives, in turn, gain their persuasive power in light of their resonance with pre-existing beliefs and traditions. Even as courts emphasize their own unique rules of evidence and argumentation, they – and the judges and lawyers who make them work – are part of the social fabric, and not outside it. At a critical moment during the rise of Nazism, a Swiss court failed, despite an appropriate opportunity, to issue a decisive repudiation of the *Protocols of the Elders of Zion*.

What, then, can and should people do to challenge recurring falsehoods, like the *Protocols*? I cannot help but observe three linked dilemmas for any who hope to take up this challenge. First, those who would challenge the falsehoods risk repeating or fueling them by engaging with them in public settings. One attractive approach is to recast the question – an option that is especially feasible in the media and the academy. The question should not be the truth or falsity of the *Protocols*, but why they continue to attract supporters despite the conclusive and repeated demonstration of their falsehood. That is the question that remains unresolved, and it also properly shifts the burden onto those who want to defend the *Protocols*.

But this points to the second dilemma: How can those who would challenge the falsehoods promote reasoned debate if they themselves are seen as evading the debate over the truth of the *Protocols*? Here, there is an eerie resemblance between the advice I have just given about recasting the question and the strategy pursued by the defendants in the *Protocols* suit in Berne. Stephen Bronner notes that the defense tried to turn the proceedings into a political trial. They tried to intimidate witnesses and to purposefully disrupt the proceedings: 'They claimed that Jews could not speak the truth and that the trial was controlled by the Jewish conspiracy.'[28] How can those who see the dissemination of the *Protocols* as a kind of conspiracy avoid both the appearance of dodging direct engagement and the tar baby of direct engagement with shifting, persistent rumor?

The third dilemma is the most difficult to resolve. How can we teach students and the broader public to be skeptical but not cynical, to tell the difference between debate and judgment, to accept complexity but not complacency? How can we help convince people that it is not only possible, but desirable, to live with complex understanding rather than simple, stereotyped claims – and at the same time, not to lose sight of simple truths?

I am reminded of the Passover Haggadah's four sons – or in the modern versions, four children. Just as the Haggadah recognizes the different kinds of audiences, so must those who want to challenge the recirculation of terrible lies about any group of people. We must recognize and speak to the one who does not even know how to ask, the one who asks a simple question, the one who sets him(or her)self up as an antagonist, and the one who is ready to embark on a deeper journey of understanding. We must learn to refute the lies, to resist engagement with those who want attention for their lies, and to invite any who would join us in the effort to resist the persistence of unfounded rumor and manufactured conspiracy theories. The genocide in Rwanda could not have occurred if people had questioned the group hatred fomented by radio broadcasts – but those broadcasts found ready ears because of the circulation and recirculation of rumors and lies. The persistence of mythologies about the past permit self-aggrandizing demagogues to tap into resentments and disappointments, by creating scapegoats and goading ordinary people into fantasies and actions of hatred and revenge.[29] The persistence of falsehoods should be a focus of study and resistance. Lives depend upon it.

NOTE

1. Alix Smith provided valuable research and editorial assistance.
2. See for example Spencie Love, *One Blood: The Death and Resurrection of Charles R. Drew* (Chapel Hill: University of North Carolina Press, 1996); Patricia Turner, *I Heard It Through the Grapevine: Rumor in African-American Culture* (Berkeley:University of California Press, 1993).
3. See for example Robert M. Baird and Stuart E. Rosenbaum, *Hatred, Bigotry, and Prejudice* (Amhurst, NY: Prometheus Books, 1999); Gordon W. Allport, *The Nature of Prejudice* (Reading, MA: Addison-Wesley, 1979, 25th anniversary edition).

4. See generally, *Protocols of the Elders of Zion: A Fabricated 'Historic' Document, a Report Prepared by the Subcommittee to Investigate the Administration of the Internal Security Act and Other Internal Security laws to the Committee on the Judiciary United States Senate* (US Government Printing Office: Washington 1964; 88th Cong. 2nd Sess.); Daniel Bourgeois, *Le Troisième Reich et la Suisse: 1933–1941* (Neuchatel: Editions de la Baconnière, 1974); Norman Cohn, *Warrant for Genocide: The Myth of the Jewish World Conspiracy and the Protocols of the Elders of Zion* (London: Serif, 1996); John S. Curtiss, *An Appraisal of the Protocols of Zion* (New York: Columbia University Press, 1942); Goran Larsson, *Fact or Fraud? The Protocols of the Elders of Zion* (Jerusalem: AMI-Jerusalem Center for Biblical Studies 1994); Frank P. Mintz, *The Liberty Lobby and the American Right* (Westport, CT: Greenwood Press, 1985); Catherine Nicault, *Le Procès des Protocoles des Sages de Sion: Une Tentative de Reposte Juive à L'Antisémitisme dans les Années 1930*, 53 *Vingtième Siècle: Revue d'Histoire* 68–84 (January-March 1997).
5. Stephen Eric Bronner, *A Rumor About the Jews: Reflections on Antisemitism and the Protocols of the Learned Elders of Zion* (New York: St. Martin's Press, 2000), pp. 76–7.
6. Ibid., pp. 83–4 (discussing Maurice Joly, *A Dialogue in Hell: Conversations Between Machiavelli and Montesquieu about Power and Right*). The plagiarized text used portions of the dialogue assigned to Machievelli to express reactionary views, even though those portions in the original version served the author's larger defense of republicanism.
7. See Cohn, *Warrant for Genocide*; Isaac Goldberg, *The So-Called 'Protocols of the Elders of Zion,' A Definitive Exposure of One of the Most Malicious Lies in History* (Girard: KS, Haldeman-Julius Publications 1936); B. W. Segel, *A Lie and a Libel: The History of the Protocols of the Elders of Zion*, trans. and ed. Richard S. Levy (Lincoln: University of Nebraska Press, 1995). See also Lucien Wolf, *The Jewish Bogey and the Forged Protocols of the Learned Elders of Zion* (London: Press Committee of the Jewish Board of Deputies, 1920).
8. See *Protocols of the Elders of Zion: A Fabricated 'Historic' Document*; Cohn, *Warrant for Genocide*; Curtiss, *An Appraisal of the Protocols of Zion*; Segal, *A Lie and a Libel*; Lucien Wolf, *The Myth of the Jewish Menace in World Affairs, or The Truth About the Forged Protocols of the Elders of Zion* (New York: Macmillan, 1921).
9. Bronner, *A Rumor About the Jews*, p 20.
10. Ibid., citing Henri Rollin, p. 2.
11. Anti-Defamation League, *Islamic Anti-Semitism in Historical Perspective* (2002), http://www.adl.org/anti_semitism/arab/Arab_Anti-Semitism.pdf (last visited 26 Feb. 2002). A former Moroccan army officer, Ahmed Rami, who fled north after a death sentence for his role in a coup attempt against King Hassan II, founded Radio Islam and featured Holocaust denial along with anti-Semitic materials, including the *Protocols of the Elders of Zion*. In October 1990, a Swedish court ruled that Rami and Radio Islam were guilty of incitement against Jews, and Rami later established Radio Islam as an Internet site. The site still exists and still distributes the *Protocols*. See http://abbc.com/islam/english/toread/pr-zion.htm (last visited1 March 2003). Amazon.com sells the book, although it includes this editorial note:

    As some readers may be aware, a hoax e-mail has been circulating widely that falsely claims Amazon.com has favorably reviewed this book. This allegation is, of course, absolutely untrue. Nevertheless, this rumor has become so widespread on the Internet that it's already a recognized 'urban legend,' just like alligators living in the sewers. Amazon.com obviously does not endorse *The Protocols of the Learned Elders of Zion*. This book is one of the most infamous, and tragically influential, examples of racist propaganda ever written. It may be useful to some as a tool in the teaching of the history of anti-Semitism, but it's unquestionably propaganda.

    Does Amazon.com sell this book? Of course we do, along with millions of other titles. *The Protocols the Learned Elders of Zion* is classified under 'controversial knowledge' in our store, along with books about UFOs, demonic possession, and all manner of conspiracy theories. You can also find books in other sections of Amazon.com's online bookstore that analyze The *Protocols*' fraudulent origins and its tragic historical role in promoting anti-Semitism and Jewish persecution, including *A Lie and a Libel: The History of the Protocols of the Elders of Zion*.

    Should Amazon.com sell *The Protocols* and other controversial works? As a bookseller, Amazon.com strongly believes that providing open access to written speech, no matter how hateful or ugly, is one of the most important things we do. It's a service that the United States Constitution protects, and one that follows a long tradition of booksellers serving as guardians of free expression in our society.

Not all countries view these issues the same way. And one of our greatest challenges is to work cooperatively with other governments to respect their laws without compromising our core values of free expression and free exchange of information – values that the Internet embodies on a global scale.

Nevertheless, Amazon.com believes it is censorship not to sell certain books because we believe their message repugnant, and we would be rightly criticized if we did so. Therefore, we will continue to make this book and other controversial works available in the United States and everywhere else, except where they are prohibited by law.

Furthermore, because we strongly believe that the appropriate response to repugnant speech is not censorship, but more speech, we will continue to allow readers, authors, and publishers to express their views about the books and other products we offer on our Web site.

We hope we have eliminated any confusion surrounding this book. If you happened to be one of the many who received the infamous e-mail, we would appreciate it if you would pass this along to your friends. It is very hurtful to everyone at Amazon.com to be accused of racism.

Thank you for your consideration.

Amazon.com, April 6 2000 Review

Although it's a pernicious fraud, *The Protocols of the Learned Elders of Zion* has unfortunately had a widespread influence – all of it evil – on the history of the twentieth century. It was exposed as a hoax in 1921, yet it has been used as a justification for the Holocaust and for innumerable pogroms in Russia and the Soviet Union.

The Protocols was supposedly written in 1897 from the minutes of 24 secret meetings between Jews and Freemasons in which they conspired to bring down Western civilization and jointly rule the world. In reality, it is nothing of the sort. In 1921, Philip Graves of the *London Times* revealed The Protocols to be a fraud, showing it to be based on a French satire aimed at Napoleon III. In a series of side-by-side extracts printed in the *Times*, Graves demonstrated that the forgers took long portions of the original text, titled *Dialogues in Hell Between Machiavelli and Montesquieu*, and simply replaced 'France' with 'Zion' and 'The Emperor' with 'We the Jews'. Further investigations by the Russian historian Vladimir Burtsev revealed other sources for *The Protocols*, including a fantasy novel by Hermann Goedsche and, more darkly, the hand of the Russian secret police.

Sadly, despite its clearly fraudulent nature, *The Protocols* continues today to feed the fears of the credulous and to fan the flames of fanaticism and hate. – Perry M. Atterberry from Amazon.com

Please note that Amazon.com does not endorse the views expressed in this book or those in the publisher's book description below.

Book Description

Translated from the Russian by Victor Marsden. This is the full-blown version, as opposed to the shorter condensed booklet we offer. Some have asked us not to offer this book. Many wish to see it banned altogether, as it claims to expose a world-wide Jewish conspiracy. We neither support nor deny its message, we simply make it available for those who wish a copy. http://www.amazon.com/exec/obidos/tg/detail/-/188539568X/qid=1046537568/sr=8-2/ref=sr_8_2/104-2571841-1295928?v=glance&s=books&n=507846#product-details.'

The customer reviews include comments supporting Amazon's contribution to free speech, comments condemning the *Protocols*, comments on the historical demonstration of the hoax— and comments supporting the *Protocols* as credible.

12. Hitler, Adolf. *Mein Kampf* (Munich: Zentralverlag der N.S.D.A.P. Franz Eher Nachf., G.M.B.H., 1935). Vol. 1; chapter XI: 'Nation and Race', pp. 307–08 (Mannheim translation).
13. John S. Curtiss, *An Appraisal of the Protocols of Zion* (New York: Columbia University Press: 1942), describesg the 1934 finding of a Swiss court at the trial of Dr A. Zander, editor of a Swiss Nazi organ that published a series of articles endorsing the *Protocols of the Elders of Zion*; J. H. Hunting, *The Protocols Of The Elders Of Zion* (reprinted from *The Vineyard*, March 1978), http://www.cdn-friends-icej.ca/antiholo/protocol.htm (a court in Grahamstown, South Africa, in August 1934 imposed fines totaling 1,.775 Rand [$4,500] on three men for concocting a modern version of the *Protocols*; Michael A. Kiltzik, 'Russian Court Rules "Protocols" An

Anti-Semitic Forgery', 28 Nov. 1993, available at www. nizkor.org/ftp.cgi?documents/protocols/protocols.001 (last visited March 1 2003)
14. Cohn, *Warrant for Genocide*, 174, 178.
15. Neil Baldwin, *Henry Ford and the Jews* (New York: St. Martin's Press, 2001).
16. *Henry Ford Invents a Jewish Conspiracy*, http://www.us-israel.org/jsource/antisemitism/ford1.html (last visited March 1 2003).
17. Ibid., pp. 177–8. See also Albert Lee, *Henry Ford and the Jews* (New York: Stein & Day, 1980).
18. Nicault, *Le Procès des Protocol*, p. 68.
19. Bronner, *A Rumor About the Jews*, pp. 120–21.
20. Curtiss, *An Appraisal of the Protocols*, p. 79 (quoting Burtsev, *Protokoly Sionskikh Mudrestov*).
21. Curtiss, ibid., p. 73.
22. Ibid., pp. 92-3 (quoting Judge Meyer, and citing Emil Raas and Georges Brunschvig, *Vernichtung einer Falschung: der Prozess um die Erfundenen 'Weisen von Zion'*, (Zurich), pp. 57–8).
23. Ibid., p. 86.
24. Ibid., p. 86-7.
25. See the eleventh *Periodic Report of States Parties* (Sweden, 18 Jan. 1993). Committee on the Elimination of Racial Discrimination (CERD/C/239/Add.1.), see State Party Report, Forty-second session, http://www.bayefsky.com/reports/sweden_cerd_c_239_add.1_1992.php (last visited March 1 2003. 'In the tenth periodic report, reference was made to a court case against Radio Islam (CERD/C/209/Add.1, paras. 32–33). Mr. Ahmed Rami, as the responsible editor for this radio programme, was convicted of persecution of a population group. The decision of the lower court was upheld by the Court of Appeal and Rami was sentenced to six months in prison. The Supreme Court has refused Mr. Rami's application for leave to appeal.'
26. Armchair Activist, http://www.jdl.org/action/armchair/radio_islam.shtml (last visited March 1 2003).
27. Michael A. Hiltzik, 'Russian Court Rules "Protocols" An Anti-Semitic Forgery'.
28. Bronner, *A Rumor About the Jews*, 120.
29. See Martha Minow, *Breaking the Cycles of Hatred*, ed. Nancy Rosenblum, Princeton, NJ: Princeton University Press 2003); Martha Minow, *Between Vengeance and Forgiveness: Facing History After Genocide and Mass Violence* (Boston, MA: Beacon Press 1998).

6

The Holocaust and Its (Re)Telling: The Nature of Evidence at the Nuremberg and Eichmann Trials

TIM COLE

When reading the account of the *Irving* v. *Lipstadt* trial written by the American journalist D. D.Guttenplan, I was particularly struck by his sense that there had been something missing from the trial – 'witnesses'. Guttenplan, in a fascinating – if problematic – section at the close of his narrative, notes a certain sympathy with the defense's decision not to call survivors as witnesses, but also a real sense of unease. By choosing not to invite survivors to take to the stand in court, Guttenplan saw nothing less than an acceptance of Irving's dismissal of survivor testimony and a retreat to the 'safety' of historical documents. Moreover, for Guttenplan, this decision meant that the trial failed in a significant respect. His argument was that, 'without witnesses, without human voices to put flesh on the facts, we have something that, while it may pass muster as history, can never tell the truth'.[1] The idea that without witnesses you have history, but not necessarily truth, is most provocative. Guttenplan suggests that 'history' is not only rather different from 'memory', but also rather different from – and I think we are to understand less than – 'truth'. The 'truth' about this event, rather than the mere 'facts' and the mere 'history', is – according to Guttenplan – to be accessed through survivor testimony. Hence his bemoaning of this particular trial, where survivor testimony was in short supply, but the expert witnesses of history were plentiful.

Reading his words reminded me of the earlier reflections of Israeli Attorney-General Gideon Hausner on what was missing from the

Nuremberg trial. Chief Prosecutor at the Eichmann trial, Hausner pointed to the consequences of the absence of witnesses at the Nuremberg trial: 'the proceedings there failed to reach the hearts of men [*sic*]').[2] The perceived failure of the Nuremberg trial to capture the imagination was remedied in the Jerusalem courtroom in 1961 with over a hundred survivors called to bear witness by the prosecution team. Their presence at this trial had a dramatic impact. In particular, they influenced both the ways in which the Holocaust narrative is told (inside as well as outside the courtroom) and the ways in which it is perceived.

I want to suggest that Guttenplan's notion that the 'truth' of the Holocaust is to be accessed through survivor testimony is representative of a particular – 'post-Eichmann trial' – historical moment. Not only was the Eichmann trial critical in the process of presenting the Holocaust as a distinct event, rather than simply one element of the Second World War, but it was also critical in creating a dominant means of representing that event: survivor testimony. In part, through the trial, the very status of those who had survived the Holocaust changed from the problematic 'displaced persons' to heroic 'survivors'.[3] Yes, parallel to the emergence of the Holocaust as the defining event of the twentieth century was the emergence of the Holocaust survivor as a legitimate narrator of the past. And both can be seen as influenced, in part, by the methodology adopted by Hausner in the Jerusalem courtroom.

The central role played by witnesses in the Eichmann trial is one element that distinguished that trial from preceding perpetrator trials, in particular the post-war trials held at Nuremberg. There are, of course, a number of significant differences between the Nuremberg trials held in Germany in the immediate aftermath of the war and the Eichmann trial held in Jerusalem in 1961. Most importantly perhaps, in the former, the Holocaust – the extermination of European Jews – was subsumed within the broader category of 'crimes against humanity', which formed only one of the charges of 'conspiracy' crimes against the 'peace' and 'war crimes' leveled against the Nazi elite in the dock. By contrast, in the latter, the focus was clearly on the 'crimes against the Jewish people', and thus the events that we know as the Holocaust were center-stage. This centrality was acknowledged in the final judgment, where the team of judges noted that,

> This is not the first time that the Holocaust has been discussed in court proceedings. It was dealt with extensively at the International Military Tribunal at Nuremberg during the trial of the Major War

> Criminals, and also at several of the trials that followed; but this time it has occupied the central place in the Court proceedings, and it is this fact which has distinguished this trial from those which preceded it.[4]

Given the centrality of the events of the Holocaust in a trial reported extensively both within Israel and internationally, the Eichmann trial has generally been seen as critical in bringing the Holocaust to the attention of a wider public.[5] However, I don't want to focus upon this particular central difference between the Nuremberg and Eichmann trials. Rather, in the light of Guttenplan's reflections on the *Irving* v. *Lipstadt* trial, I want to explore the nature of the evidence utilized by the prosecution teams in Nuremberg in 1945–46 and Jerusalem in 1961.

At Nuremberg, the documents produced by the perpetrators were deemed crucial by the prosecution team. Of the more than one hundred thousand captured German documents examined in the run-up to the trial, the prosecution chose approximately four thousand as the basis for their courtroom arguments. In preparing the case, there had been some disagreement within the American team regarding whether to present written documentary evidence primarily, or also to call witnesses. William Donovan pressed for the use of eyewitness testimony, while the Chief of Counsel Robert Jackson preferred documentary evidence.[6] Jackson's view prevailed, and in the end the prosecution only called 33 witnesses to give testimony at the trial, of which only a small number – called by the Soviet prosecution team - were Jewish victims.[7] The case was predominantly based on documentary evidence rather than witness testimony, and, in particular, on the paperwork of the perpetrators rather than the voices of the victims. These piles of documents caused one of the prosecutors, Robert Kempner, to liken these 'trials with their devastating collections of German documents' to 'the greatest history seminar ever held in the history of the world'.[8]

His words were apposite, because this body of black-and-white (rather than flesh-and-blood) evidence was seen by the prosecution team not only as sufficient to secure a prosecution, but also as the basis for an authoritative historical account. This concern was something articulated by Robert G. Storey, executive trial counsel at Nuremberg, who saw the possibility of 'the making of a record of the Hitler regime which would withstand the test of history'.[9] And what better way to ensure not only a basis for conviction, but also a basis for a future history, than through an authoritative collection of documents – the stuff of historians schooled in the Anglo-American empiricist tradition. Sir David Maxwell Fyfe (a senior member of the British prosecution team at Nuremberg) viewed these documents as an unambiguous answer to future apologist tendencies:

> Mankind produces apologists for everything; no crime is too horrible, no perversion too grotesque, for its defender not to be found; no reading of history has ever been so secure that an ingenious mind did not joyously leap into the breach to upset it. There have been no more skilled apologists than German professors and historians, and such apologists will return. Before, however, any one of them can make his case he will have to deal, not only with the judgment of the Tribunal or the speeches of the prosecution, but with the vast fortification of Nazi documents produced and examined before, and admitted by the Nazis themselves, after the fullest consideration by their counsel (Maxwell-Fyfe, 1947, p. 9).[10]

Maxwell Fyfe's words, inscribed in the foreword to one of the many books penned in the immediate aftermath of the trial, reflect the sentiments expressed by Chief British Prosecutor Sir Hartley Shawcross, when he addressed the court at the commencement of the twelfth day of the trial:

> Human memory is very short. Apologists for defeated nations are sometimes able to play upon the sympathy and magnanimity of their victors, so that the true facts, never authoritatively recorded, become obscured and forgotten ... With the passage of time the former tend to discount, perhaps because of their very horror, the stories of aggression and atrocity that may be handed down; and the latter, the credulous, misled by perhaps fanatical and perhaps dishonest propagandists, come to believe that it was not they but their opponents who were guilty of that which they would themselves condemn. And so we believe that this Tribunal, acting, as we know it will act notwithstanding its appointment by the victorious powers, with complete and judicial objectivity, will provide a contemporary touchstone and an authoritative and impartial record to which future historians may turn for truth, and future politicians for warning.[11]

For Shawcross, the ability of human memory to retain the 'true facts' – something which he saw as critical to an authoritative writing of the events of the Second World War – was questionable. In contrast to the flawed medium of memory, he saw the 'truth' that historians would demand reflected in the documentary basis to the tribunal's 'authoritative' account.

In many respects, the stated objectives of the Nuremberg trials, including securing a conviction and providing the basis for the future historiography of the Nazi period, have been attained. The documents collected for the Nuremberg trial have been consistently drawn upon in the subsequent historiography of the Holocaust. Nowhere was this more the case than in the seminal study of Raul Hilberg, which drew heavily on documents initially collected for the post-war trials.[12] Hilberg's classic text has had a profound impact on Holocaust scholarship: a scholarship that, mirroring Nuremberg, has been dominated by the history of the perpetrators rather than the victims, and has been based primarily on the paperwork produced by the perpetrators.[13]

Yet, in the same year that Hilberg's study was published in the United States, the trial of Adolf Eichmann in Israel afforded a radically different methodology. Rather than choosing to focus upon the perpetrators and present their paperwork, the prosecution team in Jerusalem chose to concentrate on the victims' stories. That is not to say that documentary evidence was absent from the Eichmann trial. Hausner acknowledged that the more than fifteen hundred documents relating to Eichmann's wartime role presented to the court – many of which had been collected at the time of the Nuremberg trials – were more than sufficient to convict Eichmann. As he himself saw it, ' in order merely to secure a conviction, it was obviously enough to let the archives speak; a fraction of them would have sufficed to get Eichmann sentenced ten times over'.[14] However, for Hausner, 'we needed more than a conviction; we needed a living record of a gigantic human and national disaster'.[15]

The Eichmann trial was intended to be about more than a 'mere' conviction, and letting the archives speak. And because of this, the mere production of documents was deemed inadequate. Hausner created a 'living record' by focusing on witnesses – flesh- and-blood Israelis. And thus the basis for proof in this trial was to differ in part from that at Nuremberg. In the Jerusalem courtroom, survivor testimony was to play a much more visible role than the textual evidence gleaned from the documents written by the perpetrators.

In short, the methodologies adopted by the prosecution teams at the Nuremberg and the Eichmann trials were radically different. As Lawrence Douglas, in a fascinating history of Holocaust trials, suggests:, the didactic paradigm of the Nuremberg Trial was the documentary – conceived either as filmic, material, or written artifact. By contrast, the representational paradigm at the Eichmann Trial was testimonial ... the representational logics of the two trials differed dramatically.[16]

During the course of the Eichmann trial, more than a hundred prosecution witnesses took the stand. Hausner intended their experiences to 'concretize' the Holocaust. In effect, this testimony shifted the focus away from Eichmann, the perpetrator, to the survivors – 'victims' and 'heroes' – whose testimony had caused such a sensation in the Jerusalem courtroom. While often seemingly peripheral to the case being tried, this victim testimony was central to the central goal of the trial, summarized by Israeli Prime Minister Ben-Gurion as a concern that 'the nations of the world ... know that there was an intention to exterminate a people' and that 'our youth remember what happened to the Jewish people. We want them to know the most tragic facts in our history.'[17]

Given the Israeli-Zionist take on the Holocaust prevalent in the 1950s and 1960s, the story told to Israeli youth and the world was to include heroism as well as martyrdom. As Ben-Gurion himself recounted in his memoirs, 'A multitude of witnesses provided shocking information on the Nazi atrocities as well as stirring facts on the heroism of the ghetto fighters.'[18] An example of the latter was the testimony given by Antek Zuckermann and Tzivia Lubetkin-Zuckerman, who had been among the leaders of the Warsaw ghetto revolt. Their testimony was tangential to the case against the man in the dock. Eichmann's 'competence and authority had been almost nil' in Poland.[19] However, their testimony was central to the narrative of the Holocaust being constructed in Israel in the 1950s and 1960s, which focused heavily on resistance in general and the Warsaw ghetto uprising in particular.[20]

But there was clearly more to this multitude of witnesses than the recounting – and in a sense reliving – of a story of martyrdom and heroism. It was not simply what they said which was significant, although the emotional impact of this flesh-and-blood testimony should not be underestimated. It was also who was saying it. The aim was that the Nation's story was to be told by the Nation – or at least as representative of a cross-section of the Nation as was possible. The act of testimony was to be a shared act, in a trial that aimed at creating a national consensus, so absent from the earlier, divisive, Kasztner Trial.[21]

In order to create a sense of nation telling a shared story, Hausner deliberately chose witnesses representative of Israeli society. From the hundreds who volunteered to give testimony, survivors were chosen not simply for the stories that they could tell, but also for who they were, given Hausner's desire to have

> the story told by a broad cross-section of the people – professors, housewives, artisans, writers, farmers, merchants, doctors, officials and laborers. That is why we called such a mixed collection of individuals to the witness box. They came from all walks of life, just as the catastrophe struck the whole nation. I asked a plumber to give evidence on the events in Bialystok, an important Jewish center. After his statement was recorded, a well-known writer, a leader of the underground in the same place volunteered to give evidence on the same events. By many standards the latter witness might have been preferable. But I wanted to have the plumber tell his story in his own simple words; so, finally, I kept him on the list and summoned him to court.[22]

This concern with who the survivors were – and what they represented – in the Israeli present, rather than only their stories of the Holocaust past, can be seen not simply in the choices of witnesses, but also in how Hausner framed their testimony. Each witness was asked to state his or her name and circumstances prior to being asked to bear witness to the past. At the conclusion of their testimony, Hausner refocused them on the present.[23] Thus these witnesses explicitly and simultaneously bore a Holocaust identity in the past and an Israeli identity in the present. Through these strategies, Hausner hoped to fuse the Holocaust past and the Israeli present in the Jerusalem courtroom. The stories of this cross-section of witnesses were intended to be the shared stories of a nation united against Eichmann and all that he represented. After the trial, Hausner suggested – with some obvious pride – that this attempt to create a sense of the nation speaking out about a shared past had been achieved:

> It came as a discovery to many that we are actually a nation of survivors. The editor of a leading newspaper told me, after listening to the shattering evidence of a woman witness in court: 'For years I have been living next to this woman, without so much as an inkling of who she was. It now transpired that almost everyone in Israel has such a neighbor.'[24]

The speaking out of survivors in the courtroom was mirrored by a more widespread speaking out of survivors throughout the country. The result was – in Haim Gouri's words – that for the first time 'in many families the true identity of the parents was now unveiled and their life story unearthed ... the Eichmann Trial heightened an awareness of the "staircase mystery" – the mystery of who your neighbor was, and where he or she came from'.[25] That speaking out, by survivors in the Jerusalem courtroom and then in the domestic space of the apartment block, was followed by a more formalized speaking out by survivors. Survivors went to the national Holocaust museum and memorial site Yad Vashem to record their stories,[26] and there was a marked rise in the number of survivor memoirs published in Israel in the aftermath of the trial.[27] Given the worldwide televised coverage of the trial, this speaking out of survivors was not restricted to Israel. In the United States, the Eichmann Trial created a 'second opening' for Holocaust survivors to speak out, after the initial short-lived window around the time of the liberation of the camps in the immediate aftermath of the war.[28]

Now, of course, there is more to the emergence of the authoritative voice – and role – of the survivor in the United States than the impact of the Eichmann trial. As Greenspan has suggested, the specific role afforded to Holocaust survivors in contemporary America owes much to a more general and 'much wider preoccupation with public and private disaster, destruction and victimization, surviving and survivalism that became pervasive in America in the 1970s'.[29] But the Eichmann trial must be seen as playing a significant role in the emergence of the survivor as *the* representative of the Holocaust. This was evident when Elie Wiesel (the survivor) replaced Anne Frank (the victim) as the representative of the Holocaust in the United States from the 1960s onwards.[30]

The impact of the Eichmann trial surpassed raising awareness of both the Holocaust as an event and Holocaust survivors as an authoritative group. This trial – which 'was a vehicle of the stories of survivors'[31] – led to survivors' testimony emerging as *the* voice through which the Holocaust narrative was told, and this, as I have suggested, owed much to the methodological choices of the prosecution team. I would go further than Douglas, who states that:

> by privileging the testimony of the survivor, the Eichmann Trial anticipated the documentary idiom of Claude Lanzmann's *Shoah*, arguably the finest film about the Holocaust, and one that notably abandons the representation logic of most documentaries by wholly eschewing the use of archival footage. By conjuring history through

word and demeanor, *Shoah* stretched the available idiom of Holocaust representation in a manner pioneered at the Eichmann Trial.[32]

I would suggest that the Eichmann trial played a significant role in influencing not simply *Shoah*, but a much more widespread series of assumptions about the dominance of survivor testimony as the means of (re)telling the story of the Holocaust. That dominance can be seen perhaps supremely in *Shoah*, but it is also present in countless other authoritative representations. Survivor testimony is the climax of the narratives offered by the Holocaust museums in Washington, DC and in Houston, Texas,[33] and the aim of Steven Spielberg's ambitious Shoah Foundation Project.

And it is here that we turn back to Guttenplan's sentiments, which, as I've suggested, are very much post-Eichmann trial sentiments. The roots of his claim that survivors offer something more than the 'history' of the event by accessing the 'truth' is not restricted to the Eichmann trial. Hausner's parade of witnesses was critical in raising the voice of the survivor as a privileged 'teller of the truth'. Not only did this trial extricate the Holocaust from the general context of the Second World War, but it also offered a particular methodology of telling this event – through the voices of the survivors. In many ways the two were inextricably linked within the context of the Jerusalem trial. The event – the Holocaust – and a dominant means of narrating the event – through survivor testimony – were in essence fused in the courtroom.

That fusion of the event and the dominant means of narrating that event underlie Guttenplan's concerns about the nature of the defense offered by Lipstadt's teams, when they chose historians' voices over those of survivors. His concerns can be historically situated as 'post-Eichmann trial' and 'pre-' a historical moment that can be dubbed 'the last of the survivors'. Guttenplan's sentiments reflect a more widespread anxiety about the death of the survivor generation.

Given the fusing of Holocaust and survivor testimony in the post-Eichmann trial period, it is not surprising that there is skepticism about whether documents alone will suffice when the last survivor dies. Guttenplan's sentiments reflect a wider set of assumptions that the 'truth' of the Holocaust cannot be made known except through survivor testimony. As I have suggested, these contemporary assumptions are, in part at least, a result of Hausner's decision to call survivors to tell the story of the Holocaust in the Jerusalem courtroom. However, the privileging of survivor testimony in telling this narrative raises the question of whether sustained (re)tellings are possible after the death of the last survivor. More importantly, there is a sense in which the Holocaust, constructed as a discrete historical event conveyed to us by survivors, is threatened by the death of the last survivor.

It is in that moment of anxiety that Guttenplan's words were written: 'Without witnesses, without human voices to put flesh on the facts, we have something that, while it may pass muster as history, can never tell the truth.' They raise the question of whether the 'truth' of the Holocaust can exist apart from its dominant means of (re)telling, that is, survivor testimony. And what is striking about that question is that it is not a question of factuality but of representation. It is not the question about whether the Holocaust happened, which is at the center of the rebuttal of Holocaust denial. Rather it is the question of how this event is (re)told, and by whom. In short, whose story is this: the historians' or the survivors'? And behind that question lies, I think, an anxiety about what happens to this story once the last survivor is gone. Should we trust only historians with the Holocaust?

NOTE

1. D .D. Guttenplan, *The Holocaust on Trial. History, Justice and the David Irving Libel Case* (London: Granta Books, 2001) pp. 306–8.
2. G. Hausner, *Justice in Jerusalem* (London: Nelson, 1967), p. 291
3. See e.g. on this process in Israel Tim Cole, *Selling the Holocaust. From Auschwitz to Schindler. How History is Bought, Packaged, and Sold* (New York: Routledge, 1999), pp. 57, 63–4.
4. L. Douglas, *The Memory of Judgment. Making Law and History in the Trials of the Holocaust* (New Haven, CT: Yale University Press, 2001) p. 98.
5. See e.g. J. E. Young, *Writing and Rewriting the Holocaust. Narrative and the Consequences of Interpretation* (Bloomington: Indiana University Press, 1990), pp. 118, 132.
6. This disagreement over the role given to eyewitness testimony was one of the reasons why Donovan ultimately left the prosecution team. See A. Tusa and J. Tusa, *The Nuremberg Trial* (London: Macmillan, 1983), p. 259; Douglas, *The Memory of Judgement*, p. 17.
7. Douglas, *The Memory of Judgment*, pp. 78–9.
8. Cited in I. Buruma, *The Wages of Guilt. Memories of War in Germany and Japan* (London: Vintage, 1994), pp. 144–5.
9. Cited in H. Arendt, *Eichmann in Jerusalem. A Report on the Banality of Evil* (New York: Viking Press, 1963), p. 253.
10. D. Maxwell Fyfe, 'Foreword' in R. W. Cooper, *The Nuremberg Trial* (Harmondsworth: Penguin, 1947), p. 9.
11. *Trial of the Major War Criminals before the International Military Tribunal. Nuremberg, 14 November 1945–1 October 1946* (Nuremberg, 1947), Vol. 3, pp. 91–2.
12. R. Hilberg, *The Destruction of the European Jews* (Chicago: Quadrangle, 1961).
13. Perhaps the most glaring example is the dominance of the so-called 'intentionalist v. functionalist' debate within Holocaust historiography in the 1980s.
14. Hausner, *Justice in Jerusalem*, p. 291.
15. Ibid.
16. Douglas, *The Memory of Judgment*, p. 104.

17. Interview in *New York Times* (December, 1960) cited in ibid., p. 57.
18. D. Ben-Gurion, *Israel. A Personal History* (New York: Funk and Wagnalls, 1971), p. 600.
19. Arendt, *Eichmann in Jerusalem*, p. 204–5.
20. See e.g. J E. Young, 'Israel's Memorial Landscape: Sho'ah, Heroism, and National Redemption' in P. Hayes (ed.), *Lessons and Legacies. The Meaning of the Holocaust in a Changing World* (Evanston: Northwestern University Press, 1991).
21. See e.g. Y. Weitz, 'The Holocaust on Trial: The Impact of the Kasztner and Eichmann Trials on Israeli Society, *Israel Studies* 1, No. 2 (1996), pp. 1–26.
22. Hausner, *Justice in Jerusalem*, p. 296.
23. Douglas, *The Memory of Judgment*, p. 165, 172.
24. Hausner, *Justice in Jerusalem*, p. 453.
25. H. Gouri, 'Facing the Glass Booth', in G. H. Hartman (ed.), *Holocaust Remembrance. The Shapes of Memory* (Blackwell: Oxford, 1994), p. 155.
26. Douglas, *The Memory of Judgment*, p. 174.
27. R. Rozett, 'Published Memoirs of Holocaust Survivors', in J. K. Roth and E. Maxwell (eds), *Remembering for the Future. The Holocaust in an Age of Genocide* (Houndmills: Palgrave, 2001), Vol. 3, p. 169.
28. G .H. Hartman, *The Longest Shadow. In the Aftermath of the Holocaust* (Bloomington: Indiana University Press, 1996), p. 143.
29. H. Greenspan, 'Imagining Survivors: Testimony and the Rise of Holocaust Consciousness', in H. Flanzbaum (ed.), *The Americanization of the Holocaust* (Baltimore, MD: Johns Hopkins University Press, 1999), p. 57.
30. Cf. P. Novick, 'Holocaust Memory in American' in J. E. Young (ed.), *The Art of Memory: Holocaust Memorials in History* (New York: Prestel, 1994), p. 162.
31. Douglas, *The Memory of Judgment*, p. 106.
32. Ibid., pp. 109–10.
33. Cole, *Selling the Holocaust*, p. 154.

7

The Surprising Historic Roots of Holocaust Denial

HENRY FEINGOLD

From the historical perspective, the denial of the Holocaust finds its roots in Allied information strategy during the Second World War. While in 1943 seventy percent of Nazi propaganda addressed the Jewish question, the fate of the Jews in Nazi- occupied Europe was rarely mentioned in Allied propaganda. Political leaders and officials high in the government bureaucracies in Washington and London initially refused to believe the news leaking out of occupied Europe and, after the genocide was confirmed in the fall of 1942, they often continued to deny it. That is the setting for one of the bitterest ironies of the war, that there is no mention of this bloodiest of all war crimes in the charter under which major Nazi war criminals were tried in Nuremberg. Not until the trial of Adolf Eichmann in 1962 was that unwillingness to confront Hitler's 'final solution', as a separate and specific crime, reversed. The suppression of the gruesome story of the Nazi implementation of its 'final solution' was not always intentionally evil. Some reasons are related to wartime strategy. But for purposes of this discussion we need to take note of a great paradox: Holocaust denial began with the 'good guys', in order, it was imagined, to better wage a 'just war' against an enemy obsessed with the liquidation of the Jewish people.

Athough it involved nothing less than converting the industrial process that distinguished advanced life on earth to the mass production of death, a researcher in the archives still experiences considerable difficulty in finding a written record of how the genocide of the Jews was planned and implemented. That scarcity of evidence that documents the disappearance of millions doesn't mean that Allied leaders were unaware of it. A fairly comprehensive picture of the workings of the 'final solution' was available to Allied governments. There was an early ability to read the 'decrypts' of reports transmitted by SS killing units; there were underground sources linked to the governments in exile; there was an industrialist close to Nazi authorities whose information was included in the famous Riegner cable; in later years there was the report of two escaped death camp inmates; and there were Vatican sources who received information from the Church's extensive parish network, which included the death camps in Poland.

The news of the implementation of the 'final solution' was variously suppressed, ignored or trivialized partly to lessen the impact on public opinion, which, it was feared, would lead to increased pressure for a change of Allied war priorities to include retribution, especially through bombing. Such pressure by the governments in exile later compelled Anthony Eden, the British Foreign Minister, to suggest the convening of another refugee conference in inaccessible Bermuda in March 1943. Not only did the US State Department attempt to make certain, after the Riegner cable had substantiated the mass murder plans, that no more such news should be received in its diplomatic pouch, it also developed a euphemistic vocabulary during the refugee phase to conceal the effects of Berlin's extrusion and deportation policy. The three governmental agencies created to respond to Berlin's actions – the Intergovernmental Committee on Political Refugees (IGCPR), the President's Advisory Committee on Political Refugees (PACPR) and the War Refugee Board (WRB) – never revealed that the word 'refugees' referred largely to the Jewish victims of Berlin's strenuous efforts to make the Reich *Judenrein*. While Berlin was converting all potential enemies, including Roosevelt, to the Jewish faith, Washington was using the neutral classification of 'refugee' to conceal the Jewish character of the crisis. As late as the acceptance of the temporary haven idea, suggested by the *New York Post* columnist Samuel Grafton in the spring of 1944, Roosevelt's special emissary in North Africa, Robert Murphy, received instructions to select 'reasonable proportions' of ethnic refugees to avoid the impression that the government was in the business of rescuing Jews.

The information strategy based on avoidance and concealment of the crime also prevailed in London. The Holocaust was never allowed to become part of the ongoing discussions at the major wartime conferences that determined war aims and strategy. There is no record to indicate that

Churchill ever discussed it with Roosevelt at their several private meetings during the war. Most astounding, what was being done to the Jews of Europe was not a topic of deliberation by the United Nations War Crimes Commission (UNWCC), which started its discussions in 1942 and continued throughout the war. The 'final solution' was not mentioned in the several Allied declarations concerning war crimes. The first such statement, the St James Declaration dealing with war crimes issued by the governments in exile on April 18 1940, mentioned the destruction of the Polish nation and the 'atrocious treatment' of the Jews, among other groups. Throughout the war the British Foreign Office was adamantly opposed to statements of retribution, although Britain had ample evidence of the effectiveness of this in the shackling of the prisoner of war (POW) issue that came up after Dunkirk. Finally, under pressure from the governments in exile, Eden, speaking for 11 Allied governments, acknowledged that Germany was following a policy of extermination against Jews. On the middle level, officials continued to disbelieve it.

Finally, Roosevelt induced Churchill and Stalin to allow him to issue a declaration that spoke of putting war criminals on trial when peace came. But it was by no means certain on December 17 1942, when the declaration was proclaimed, that it would be a peace that the Allies imposed on the Axis powers, nor was the specific crime against the Jews mentioned. In 1943, in fact, the death camps continued to function at full speed. After much agitation, the matter of German war crimes finally was included on the agenda of the meeting of foreign ministers in Moscow scheduled for November 1943. The Moscow Declaration on war crimes that followed also neglected to mention the 'final solution'. Instead, a procedure for trying major war criminals by tribunals in each country was established. Of course, the Jews of Europe who bore the brunt of Nazi savagery had no such country, and were therefore left out of the search for justice that would come with the peace. The omission of crimes against Jews was not an oversight. Speaking of the suggestion by Jewish organizations that they should be allowed to participate in the discussions to establish the UNWCC, Roger Allen, an official in the British Foreign Office, stated openly that: 'It is, I think, agreed that we should resist such proposals.' In a word, the 'final solution' was treated as a non-happening.

At the same time, the Soviets who bore the brunt of German atrocities rejected the strictures of international law when considering German war crimes. To Churchill's chagrin, Stalin suggested at the

Teheran Conference that 50,000 German officers should simply be summarily shot. Stalin later claimed that he was not serious, but that was in fact frequently the way the matter was settled on the eastern front. Roosevelt was finally prepared to discuss the war crimes issue at the Yalta Conference of February 1945, including the now undeniable genocide operation against the Jews, but it was never broached, since, if anything, Stalin was not anxious to discuss the question of the fate of the Jews as it would have reinforced Nazi propaganda efforts to link communism and Judaism under the rubric *Judeobolshevism*. In the post-war era, the Soviet bloc nations continued to spare no effort to conceal the fact that the target of the genocide was the Jews. The war memorials at mass execution sights such as Babi Yar in the Ukraine do not call attention to the fact that the victims were Jews. Jews became in death what they had rarely been allowed to be in life – honored citizens of the nation.

As word of German excesses began to leak out of Europe, particularly after the Lidice massacre in June 1942, pressure increased in Washington and London to issue some kind of statement that would indicate Allied awareness of German depredations in the occupied countries. The governments in exile particularly wanted to transmit the notion that war crimes, as explicated in the Geneva Convention, were being monitored and that perpetrators would be held accountable. But when German arms were everywhere victorious in the early years of the war, such threats of retribution would have been considered empty gestures. After Russia's decisive victory at Stalingrad in the early months of 1943 and its defeat in the decisive battle of Kursk, Germany's defeat became a matter of time. However, the efforts of the Nazi regime to win the war against the Jews, a war that could still be won, actually grew more determined.

As the barbarism of German occupation policy in the East became fully manifest, the Polish government in exile requested that the early raids in 1942 against German cities such as Cologne be projected in Allied propaganda as retribution for Nazi atrocities in Poland. However, the ghettoization of the Jews and early knowledge of the death camps were not mentioned, since, for the Polish government, the victims were simply Polish citizens. The harsh treatment of Jews was not differentiated as part of a genocide operation. The Poles continued to insist on a statement linking German criminality in the East to the savaging of German cities from the air. But by the spring of 1943, aside from the desultory Italian campaign, the air war against German cities was the only major Allied contribution to the war effort. Several of the highest officials of the British government, including Churchill, supported such an information strategy. But it did not prevail over the opposition of the military and of middle echelon officials, who for various reasons, including legal prohibitions embedded in the Geneva Convention, would not implement such a policy. The reluctance to broach the question of the 'final solution' in the Allied camp was especially strong within the group of international law experts who were still haunted by the failure to bring German war criminals to justice in the Leipzig trials after the First World War (May 1921). Many international law experts were concentrated in government legal departments on both sides of the Atlantic, and most were opposed to the very idea of trials and retribution.

Even for those who honor the law above all else, there cannot help but be a sense of frustration about prohibiting the use of legal strictures against acts of revenge in international law to stay the hand of a society that had turned to genocide. The Allied rejection of a strategy that required acknowledgment of genocide has become a point of contention in the historical debate, since making such information available might have opened up the question of the 'final solution'. A statement that the bombing of a German city was the first installment of a policy of retribution for what was being done in the name of the German people would have created enormous problems for the failing German war effort. However strong the support for Hitler may have been in all social strata of the German population, by 1943, as the casualties in the East began to mount and the destruction of thousands of homes and civilian casualties by a round-the clock bombing campaign became apparent, support for a genocide program that was totally extraneous to winning the war would surely not have been able to maintain popular support if Germans had realized that the price of the 'final solution' was the lives of their dear ones. That may have been the real reason why talk of what was being done to the Jews in the east by returning soldiers was punishable by death.

The deportation and disappearance of millions could not, of course, be concealed indefinitely. Indeed, by the final months of 1942, Allied governments were well aware that a world of concentration camps in which thousands of people were entombed dotted occupied Europe, and that six of these camps were devoted exclusively to processed killing. There were also massive deportations and the recruitment of slave labor forced to live under brutal conditions. The urgency to establish an agency to monitor these unprecedented trespasses of the long-established rules of war was considered imperative. Some believed that the mere existence of such an agency would help to curb German excesses. The governments in exile that represented the nations under German occupation could keep a watchful eye on such matters as mass killing or slave labor. Who would watch out for those who were bearing the brunt of the murderous policy based on imagined eugenic enhancement? Predictably, open season could be, and was, declared on Jews who were without legal and political protection until the establishment of the Jewish state in 1948.

The agency whose development may serve as a prism through which to observe the legal and political factors that went into the unwillingness of the Allies to address the Holocaust directly can be found in the United Nations War Crimes Commission. By the early months of 1942 there was general agreement that such a special agency to handle the war crimes problem was needed. But not until October 1943, after a year of bickering, was the UNWCC formally established. From the outset, the new international agency faced difficult problems in handling news of massive and unprecedented German atrocities, growing out of the Nazi concept of *vernichtungskrieg* (total destruction of the enemy), which they waged in the east and in which the death camp was incubated. Soviet POWs were the earliest victims of the gas chambers at Auschwitz. As in the case of rescue of Jews, the opposition to dealing with war crimes generally, and the Holocaust specifically, emanated from the British Foreign Office and the US State Department. The object of both agencies was to neutralize the activities of such an effort while at the same time creating the impression, for the governments in exile and the increasingly aroused British public opinion, that something was being done. The planned murder of an entire people through a policy called the 'final solution' was projected in the public arena as an ordinary war crime yet to be substantiated, that would be dealt with together with other crimes when peace came. But it soon became apparent that Hitler's prime target for total annihilation, the Jews, could somehow not be considered apart from other lesser atrocities. Somehow trying to place a brake on Nazi genocide policy through threats of retribution was not considered, although it was clear as early as the summer of 1943 that Germany would lose the war and therefore become more amenable to negotiations.

At two junctures in the troubled relations of his administration to the Holocaust, Roosevelt turned to his old school cronies to bypass the State Department, for which he had little use. In 1938, soon after the unsuccessful Evian Conference, he called upon George Rublee, who had played a role in settling a former oil dispute with Mexico, to bring some order to the refugee chaos created by Berlin's extrusion policy. The negotiations were successful, but many considered the results a kind of ransom proposal for the release of hostage Jewish communities in Germany and Austria. Again, after the flouting of the rules of war regarding the treatment of prisoners both in the European and Pacific theaters of war, Roosevelt turned to a Harvard school friend, Robert (Birdie) Pell, who had served in Congress from an upstate New York district and had helped the 1936 Roosevelt campaign. After that campaign, Pell turned to his friend in the White House for a job. To the dismay of the professionals in the State Department, Pell was granted a position as minister to Portugal in 1937, and in 1941 he was posted to the American diplomatic delegation in Budapest, which allowed him to witness first hand the precarious condition of the Jews in central Europe. What dismayed the State Department was that Pell, like other 'old friends', maintained a personal correspondence with Roosevelt that he did not hesitate to use to gain political leverage. He frequently boasted of his access to the Oval Office.

After Budapest, Pell asked for and received an appointment to the American delegation to the UNWCC, which had finally been established in October 1943. He aspired to become chairman of the commission, but his tenure would last barely two years. The nub of the conflict lay in Pell's strong conviction that the unprecedented ferocity of the Nazi crimes in occupied Europe required a broadening of international law and a specific reference to crimes against the Jewish people. That flew in the face of the prevailing opinion, both in the State Department and Foreign Office, not to deal with war crimes.

For a while it seemed that Pell might prevail. He insisted that one of the grounds for indictment should be crimes committed against a nation's own citizens, dating back to 1933. While not mentioning Jews directly, such crimes dealt with the depredations committed against German Jewry, such as *Kristallnacht* of November 9 and 10 1938, and the coerced expropriation and forced sale of Jewish property. Pell did win an indirect victory before his resignation. He frequently wrote to Roosevelt apprising him of the developments on the war crimes issue, and used the occasion to warn of the political consequences of permitting the moral lapses inherent in State Department war crimes policy to continue unchecked. It seemed to work. By 1944, the President who in 1939 would not support the Wagner–Rogers Bill to permit 20,000 Jewish refugee children to enter the country outside the quota system, now made several direct mentions of crimes against the Jews, and on January 20 1944 signed a directive creating the War Refugee Board. The activities of the board, especially in the Hungarian phase of the Holocaust, marked the zenith of the American rescue effort. Two months later Roosevelt approved the idea of Free Ports, dubbed temporary havens by the State Department, which brought almost a thousand refugees to Oswego, New York, outside the immigration laws. But on the war crimes issue, Roosevelt, preoccupied with the conduct of the war and with worsening health, reverted to passivity. The war crimes issue, in which the Holocaust was embedded, was allowed to fall back under the control of the experts in the State Department, who were able to rid themselves of Pell by simply neglecting to request an appropriation for his position. He left the UNWCC in January 1945.

Roosevelt's support proved to be chimerical. The charter on which the Nuremberg war crimes trials were based grew out of the UNWCC's work. The massive genocidal act against the Jewish people (the term Holocaust did not come into use until several years after the war) was not directly considered at Nuremberg. Instead, the crimes associated with the 'final solution' became part of the broader charge included in the 'crimes against humanity' provision of the Charter. Not until the Jewish state captured and tried Adolf Eichmann, 16 years later, did the dreadful fate of European Jewry enter public consciousness, where it has remained ever since. It is that presence, and the justice it demands, which is the source of David Irving's problem.

Ironically, there is some reason to believe that the speedy recognition of Israel by the United States and the Soviet Union was partly based on a rare feeling of contrition for what had befallen the Jews of Europe. It created a 'window of opportunity' for the establishment of the Jewish state. It was that state which broke through the denial and concealment of what had happened by placing Eichmann on trial. There were portents before the revelations at the trial that the time for turning a blind eye to the Holocaust had passed. The public reaction to the Harrison report in 1947 on the condition of Jewish displaced persons (DPs), who were often housed in the same barracks with their tormentors, was one such example. The fateful plight of ships like the *Exodus* in carrying hundreds of survivors to Palestine was another. Truman ordered the separate housing and treatment of Jewish DPs within the camps themselves. Today that separation marks the first public recognition that the Holocaust was not an ordinary war crime and that Jews did, in fact, face a programmed murder as part of German public policy during the war.

Yet despite the revelations and the photos of piles of corpses, the resistance to dwell on the atrocities and to seek some form of accounting persisted. The Cold War meant that the sense of national threat, associated for years with Berlin, was now linked to Moscow. The trial of German war criminals, some believed, ran against the American national interest, because Germany would be needed as an ally. The opposition to the Eichmann trial a decade later, like the denial of a separate venue for the consideration of war crimes against Jews, continued to be couched in legal terms. At the trial, the defense counsel cited international law experts who maintained that the capture and trial of Eichmann was clearly *ex post facto* and therefore illegal, since Israel did not exist at the time when these crimes were committed. The Israeli government went through great pains to meet these challenges to the trial's legality. The court did not convene until eight months after Eichmann's capture in May 1960, to allow time for preparation of the trial, including research in all relevant archives, except those of the Soviet Union to which researchers were denied access. The trial itself lasted five months, and an additional eight months passed to allow the appeals to go forward. Eichmann was finally executed on May 3 1962. To counter the charge of illegality, Israel again argued that she was a recognized successor agency for the destroyed Jewish community of Europe. A community that had already been recognized by the Chancellor of West Germany, Konrad Adenauer, when he signed the first reparations agreement with Israel in 1952. Moreover, the 'Crimes Against Humanity' and the 'Membership In A Criminal Organization' provisions of the Nuremberg War Crimes Charter allowed any nation-state to apprehend and try war criminals. Domestically, too, Israel had laid the legal groundwork for the Eichmann trial by placing a 'Nazi Collaborator Punishment Law' in its criminal code in 1950.

From the perspective of Holocaust denial, what was crucial about the Eichmann trial was that it acted as a corrective to the Nuremberg trials, whose charter was based on Allied denial that a separate category of crime had been committed against the Jewish people. Eichmann was specifically tried for 'Crimes Against the Jewish People'. Had deniers had their way the Holocaust would have been forgotten, lost in the countless atrocities of a particularly cruel war. The Eichmann trial also relates directly to the failure of David Irving's libel charge against Deborah Lipstadt. The government of Israel permitted the secret thousand-page tell-all memoir that Eichmann voluntarily wrote while in custody to be used by the defense.

It needs to be emphasized that the denial embedded in Allied wartime information strategy and David Irving's denial are not cut from the same cloth. The legal rationale for underplaying the Jewish question during the war was that the Jews were not represented by a recognized state, but were citizens of the states in which they resided, including the Reich. In fact, the legal reason was throughout overshadowed by the strategic reason for Allied denial and avoidance of the Holocaust. If the Allies addressed the Nazi propaganda construct called the 'Jewish question', it would inevitably give Berlin a bargaining chip while interfering with the war effort at home. Jews were not winning medals for popularity, and a nation reluctant to go to war would become more so if Berlin maneuvered Allied propaganda into publicizing war aims that included one to save the Jews.

Contemporary denial such as Irving's is a form of anti-Semitism that seeks to delegitimize the Jewish presence in history. It wants to undermine communal identity, a threat to which Jews are especially vulnerable, since through much of their history they lived without a land of their own and have become dependent on historical memory for communal cohesion. Who composes a community's history, and what its content will be, depends on the play of power. A community deprived of power cannot write its own history. The establishment of the Jewish state once again allowed Jews to regain control or to 're-enter' history, as Zionist ideologues put it. That is what the Eichmann trial corrective is all about. History – especially Jewish history – before the Jewish state was a battlefield related directly to the Jew's group identity. Losing one's place on the historical canvas, as Jews well know, is the first step to communal oblivion. That is also the reason why the growth of Holocaust denial in the Arab world is particularly disturbing. The conflict between Arab and Jew is not only about land, it is about historical memory and therefore at its very core it is an existential conflict.

Whether by commission or omission, historical falsification can never be an innocent exercise. There is always a price to be paid for such falsification. Contemporary Holocaust denial is the price we pay for Allied unwillingness to reveal the truth about what role the Jewish question played in the waging of that very bloody war. History may not be able to reveal the entire truth, but over time it acts as a great sorter outer. It has taken time to piece together the tampered-with historical record of the war and what led up to it. But each year, as the archives are opened wider, we learn more. Contemporary historiography of the war pays much more attention to the Holocaust than the history written during the fifties and sixties. As the war progressed and the light of victory could be seen at the end of the tunnel, the gates of the camps were opened and the ghastly sight within was witnessed by the public. In itself that established a new datum that changed the historical story fashioned, in some measure, by the information strategy of the Office of War Information (OWI), the British Foreign Office and the State Department. But the total defeat of Holocaust denial awaits the historical narrative that will finally present a balanced picture of the role of Hitler's 'Jewish question' in bringing on and shaping the terrible character of that war. We learn that an Auschwitz is what can happen when an obsession is clothed in the power of the state. In his suicide note written in the bunker, Hitler spoke not about the need for *lebensraum* in the east, one of the Reich's geopolitician's favorite justification for waging aggressive war. He did not even mention the injustice of the Treaty of Versailles. Rather he wrote of the need to destroy the Jews. It was central to his view of the world and for that reason alone it will become more important in the way historians are reconsidering the war. In a word we are moving in the opposite direction of Holocaust denial. That case too is being lost by David Irving.

To the Nuremberg and Eichmann Trials that frame this discussion there now needs to be added the libel trial of Deborah Lipstadt. The latter two trials do something rare in history, they offer correctives through the courts rather than through the free development of historiography. It may be that from an historical perspective the hero in history is one who succeeds in removing a fallacy from the historical narrative. If that is true, then David Ben Gurion, the Prime Minister of Israel who was the driving force behind the capture and trial of Eichmann and who foresaw its corrective aspect, surely qualifies as one. Paradoxically, the second case, the recent trial for libel of Deborah Lipstadt, yields no similar heroic actor. Here, the corrective was given to us through an act of perversity by David Irving, who brought suit against Deborah Lipstadt for libel. (Those who have noted the same radical contrariness in his other historical writings were not surprised.) From the perspective of Jewish history, both trials are acts of redemption. If Jews had been satisfied with the Nuremberg war crimes trials, the destruction of European Jewry would have become merely another atrocity in a particularly cruel war. The historical memory would have been lost, and David Irving would have won his case.

Finally, while it is difficult to speak of progress when examining such events, there is a hopeful contemporary resonance that allows us to imagine that we have become better than we were. The concepts of international law that proved to be so inadequate in confronting the massive crime of genocide have been considerably strengthened. Today, potential criminal leaders should not contemplate 'ethnic cleansing' with impunity. But more important than the expansion of the reach of international law is the emergence of a justice-seeking community that monitors human trespasses. In some small way Deborah Lipstadt's victory over David Irving in this trial is part of that. The accounting is not perfect, as the inadequate response to the mass murders in Rwanda attest, but it is a beginning, and life on earth for those who cannot quite fit in is in some small way more secure.

SELECTED BIBLIOGRAPGHY

Arendt, Hannah, *Eichmann In Jerusalem: A Report on the Banality of Evil*, New York: Viking Press, 1964.

Bard, Mitchell G., *Forgotten Victims: The Abandonment of Americans in Hitler's Camps*, Boulder: West View Press, 1994.

Bartov, Omer, *The Eastern Front, German Troops, and the Barbarization of Warfare*, New York: St Martin's Press, 1986.

Breitman, Richard, *Official Secrets: What the Nazis Planned, What the British and Americans Knew*, New York: Hill and Wang, 1998.

Burleigh, Michael, *The Third Reich: A New History*, New York: Hill and Wang, 2000.

Dallek, Robert, *Franklin D. Roosevelt and American Foreign Policy, 1932–1945*, New York: Oxford University Press, 1979.

Davidson Eugene, *The Trial of the Germans: An Account of the Twenty Two Defendants Before the International Miliary Tribunal at Nuremberg*, New York: Macmillan Press, 1966.

Dinnerstein, Leonard, *Antisemitism in America*, New York: Oxford University Press, 1994.

'The Eichmann Trial: The Proceedings,' *American Jewish Yearbook*, 1962, New York: 1962.

Engel, David, *Facing a Holocaust: The Polish Government-in-Exile and the Jews, 1939–1942*, Chapel Hill: University of North Carolina Press, 1987.

— Facing a Holocaust: *The Polish Government-in-Exile,1943–1945*, New York: New York University Press, 1993.

Feingold, Henry L., *The Politics of Rescue: The Roosevelt Administration and the Holocaust, 1938–1945*, New York : Oxford University Press, 1979 (pp. 186–93).

— 'Bombing Auschwitz and the Politics of the Jewish Question During

World War II,' in *The Bombing of Auschwitz: Should the Allies Have Attempted It?*, Michael Neufeld and Michael Berenbaum, Eds. New York: St Martin's Press, 2000.
— *Bearing Witness: How America and Its Jews Responded to the Holocaust*, Syracuse: Syracuse University Press, 1995.
Gilbert, Martin, *Auschwitz and the Allies: How the Allies Responded to the News of Hitler's Final Solution*, New York: Holt, Rhinehart and Winston, 1981.
Hausner, Gideon,, *Justice In Jerusalem*, New York: Harper and Row, 1966.
Kennedy, David, *Freedom From Fear: The American People In Depression and War*, 1929–1945, New York: Oxford University Press, 1999.
— *I Will Bear Witness: A Diary of the Nazi Years*, Vol. I, *1933–1941*, Vol. II, *1942-1945*, New York: Oxford University Press, 1998 and 1999.
Kochavi, Arieh J., *Prelude To Nuremberg: Allied War Crimes Policy and the Question of Punishment*, Chapel Hill: University of North Carolina Press, 1998.
Laqueur, Walter, *The Terrible Secret : Suppression About Hitler's 'Final Solution,'* Boston: Little Brown, 1980.
Lochner, Louis P., ed. *The Goebbels Diaries, 1942–1943*, New York: Garden City Doubleday, 1948.
Medoff, Rafael, *The Deafening Silence*, New York: Shapolsky Publishers, 1987.
Segev, Tom, *The Seventh Million: The Israelis and the Holocaust*, New York: Hill and Wang, 1993.
Winkler, Allen M., *The Politics of Propaganda: The Office of War Information*, New Haven and London: Yale University Press, 1978.

8

Jewish Victims in a Wartime Frame: A Press Portrait of the Nuremberg Trial

LAUREL LEFF

In the fall of 1945, German atrocities captured the American public's attention as they never had before and never would again. The Second World War was over and the Cold War had not yet begun. Searing images from the liberated concentration camps remained vivid in the minds of Americans who had seen the newsreels in the darkness of first-run movie theaters. An international trial of top Nazi leaders, just under way in Nuremberg, promised a modicum of retribution for the agonies of the previous six years.

At that critical moment,[1] Germany's crimes were presented as having little to do with the systematic campaign to obliterate Europe's Jews. The Nuremberg trials, which dominated all discussions of post-war justice and shaped Americans' views for decades to come, relegated the Holocaust to a footnote. The trials' primary text described Germany's brutal war of aggression, mentioning only secondarily and generally the many helpless peoples ensnared in the fatherland's quest for world domination.[2] As a result, legal scholar Lawrence Douglas argues, the Nuremberg trials failed to 'do justice to the history of the Holocaust'. Doctrinal interpretations and prosecutorial maneuverings dictated the trials' contours, and consequently shaped post-war perceptions. 'The legal grid in which unprecedented atrocities were framed', Douglas contends in his important book, *The Memory of Judgment: Making Law and History in the Trials of the Holocaust,* contributed to the 'serious shortcoming in the historical understanding of the Holocaust that emerged from Nuremberg.'³ Historian Michael Marrus has a less harsh assessment. In his view the trials presented enough evidence of the 'Nazis' anti-Jewish policy' to provide 'a full account of the massacres of European Jewry', and to lay the documentary foundation that enabled the Holocaust to emerge in its own right years later. Yet Marrus also acknowledges that 'because the trial was such a prodigious affair ... information about [the Holocaust] easily could be drowned in the greater flood of crimes and accusations.'⁴

In all the analyses of Nuremberg's legacy, one explanation for the Holocaust's submergence has been largely overlooked.⁵ Prosecutors presented the evidence of crimes against the Jews in the court of Law, but the press presented it to the court of public opinion. Throughout the trials, the press furnished 'the window through which our doings were observed in the outside world,' Telford Taylor, associate counsel, observes in his memoirs.⁶ The American press provided more than a portal for observing the trials' key events, however.⁷ Through decisions about what to include, what to exclude, what to emphasize and what to ignore, the press not only accepted the prosecution's depiction of German crimes as those primarily of aggressive war, it in fact accentuated that portrayal. By conveying this image to the public, the press contributed to what Henry L. Feingold describes as a form of Holocaust denial – the 'unwillingness to reveal the truth about what role the Jewish question played in the waging of that very bloody war'. The press therefore both influenced contemporaneous understanding of the Holocaust and helped to shape Americans' short-term memory of that event.

I intend to make that argument by examining the *New York Times*' coverage of the Nuremberg trials of 22 senior German officials that began in November 1945 and ended in October 1946. I selected the *Times* for two reasons. First, the *Times* was one of the few American newspapers to maintain a presence in the courtroom and to publish daily stories throughout the trial.⁸ Others newspapers relied on the wire services, and reported just the start of the trial, the announcement of the verdicts and the defendants' executions.⁹ Second, the *Times* had unparalleled influence on the American public, both because of its own reach and because of its effect on opinion-makers. In the mid-1940s, the *Times* came closer to being a national newspaper than any of its competitors.¹⁰ More important, policy-makers and other journalists looked to the *Times* for guidance. '[T]he New York *Times* has more than ever established itself as the foremost daily of the world,' the respected former editor of *The Nation*, Oswald Garrison Villard, wrote in a 1944 book of press criticism. 'No important journalist can possibly do without it, and it has literally made itself indispensable to anyone who desires to be thoroughly informed as to what is happening on this globe.'[11] I will present my argument in three stages: first, I will discuss the trials' legal framework as it relates to German crimes against the Jews; second, I will examine how the press presented the legal argument to the public; and third, I will suggest reasons why the press portrayed the trials as it did.

When the Nuremberg trials opened, chaos reigned in post-war Germany. Millions wandered the highways: former combatants whose services were no longer needed; ex-slave laborers who were on their way home; Jews who had no home to which they could return. Germany's bombed-out cities had little food, water, or electricity. Corpses rotted under the rubble while families lived on top. Journalists were as overwhelmed as every one else as they struggled to explain the enormity of the destruction and to assess the possibility of reconstruction.[12] In the midst of this mess, the war crimes trials promised order, not only in the abstract sense of restoring the rule of law, but also in the concrete sense of providing a structured story. For journalists, trials have a satisfying narrative arc: they open, they close, with moments of drama (and tedium) in between. Most important, they give resolution in the form of a verdict. The Nuremberg trials had the additional allure of offering an explanation for the cataclysm the world had just endured.[13]

About 250 journalists from 20 countries, including roughly 80 American correspondents, flocked to Nuremberg – at the time the largest group ever to cover one event.[14] The International Military Tribunal hearing the case accommodated the journalists, reserving the best seats right behind the prosecution in the Palace of Justice, providing a vast press room to which the proceedings were piped via loudspeakers, and even billeting them in a nearby castle under US Army auspices. Among the reporters were a half-dozen from the *New York Times*, who covered the trials at one time or other.[15] Leading the pack was Raymond Daniell, who had been the *Times* London bureau chief during most of the war. Backing him up was his wife and fellow *Times* London correspondent, Tania Long, who had grown up in Berlin where her father had been the *Times* financial correspondent. A sign of the importance the *Times* attached to Daniell's assignment was that every article he wrote on the trials bore his byline – then a novelty for a news story.

When Daniell and his fellow journalists descended on depleted Nuremberg, the trials' parameters had already been set.[16] From their opening on 21 November 1945, the charge of aggressive war – the planning, initiating and waging of war in violation of international treaties – was the centerpiece. Although only one of four charges – the others being war crimes, crimes against humanity and conspiracy to commit the other three – the aggressive war charge came to dominate the proceedings, both because of the way in which the indictment was framed and the way the case was tried. Germany's campaign to destroy European Jewry most easily fit within the rubric of the third count, crimes against humanity, which included murder, extermination, enslavement and deportation of civilian populations, and encompassed persecution on political, racial and religious grounds. How these crimes differed from war crimes, instead of being atrocities against military personnel and civilians in violation of the Hague and Geneva Conventions, was never carefully delineated, except to the extent that they were carried out behind the front lines. But the International Military Tribunal, made up of judges from the four prosecuting nations, restricted the reach of crimes against humanity. It ruled that only those crimes against humanity committed in connection with the other two substantive counts, aggressive war or war crimes, fell within its jurisdiction. That meant that the prosecution would have to prove that the Germans murdered Jews as part of a criminal war of aggression, or as a war crime. The tribunal further subsumed the extermination campaign within the aggressive war charge by a ruling on the one non-substantive count. That count, common plan or conspiracy, charged the defendants with organizing a conspiracy to commit the other crimes. The tribunal held, however, that the conspiracy count specified only one separate crime – a conspiracy to commit acts of aggressive war. The indictment did not encompass conspiracy to commit war crimes, or conspiracy to commit crimes against humanity. '[T]he conspiracy charge was constructed in such a way as to *limit*, rather than extend, the reach of crimes against humanity, which ... had already been parsed as itself dependent on the aggressive war charge,' Douglas explains. The upshot: the crimes against the Jews, if they were to be presented at all, would be as part of the crime of aggressive war.[17]

The way the prosecution tried the case further obscured the extermination campaign aimed at the Jews. Each country presented a part of the case: the Americans handled the conspiracy count; the British, aggressive war; the French and Russians took on war crimes and crimes against humanity, with the French focusing on transgressions in the west, the Russians, on violations in the east. The Americans went first. This meant that the count of conspiracy to wage aggressive war was heard when interest in the trial was at its peak. During the first three weeks, the prosecution presented a detailed history of the origins of the Second World War – the failure of the Munich peace talks, the annexation of the Sudetenland, the Austrian Anchluss, even Pearl Harbor. In the third week, prosecutors moved on to demonstrate how war crimes and crimes against humanity were part of that conspiracy. But even in that section of the Americans' case, which would seemingly address crimes against the Jews, the prosecutors' presentation minimized the Holocaust.

Douglas illustrates how that happened through a penetrating discussion of the *Nazi Concentration Camp* film. (The *Times*' coverage of the film's screening is also revealing, as I will explain later.) At first blush, the prosecution's decision to show the film two weeks into the trial appears perplexing. The overwhelming images of Nazi atrocities would seem likely to at least dwarf, and potentially to derail, the discussion of aggressive war. And the film – which has since been used in other trials and in fictionalized accounts of Nuremberg as 'irrefutable evidence of the Holocaust' – would seem to bring crimes against the Jews to center stage. Yet the film's narrators do not appear to be documenting the atrocities against the Jews, Douglas contends. Indeed, the film mentions the word 'Jew' just once, and in a way that suggests Nazi violence did not target Jews as a group. 'The 4,000 Ohrdruf [concentration camp] victims are said to include Poles, Czechs, Russians, Belgians, Frenchmen, German Jews and German political prisoners,' the film's narrator intones. Elsewhere, the narration identifies the piles of corpses and emaciated bodies as those of 'political prisoners', 'Belgian patriots', slave laborers, prisoners of war, or 'surviving inmates ... representing every European nationality.' To Douglas, the film's narration confirms the broader legal strategy: 'By framing its horrific scenes in a narrative about perverted militarism and the excesses of war and by sweeping together evidence of the final solution with evidence of conventional war crimes, the film delivered a vision of Nazi atrocity fully consonant with the prosecution's case,' he argues. 'Just as the final solution was, in the documentary's eye, indistinguishable from atrocities against political prisoners and POWs, so crimes against humanity, as a legal matter, were absorbed into a conventional understanding of war crimes. In this way, the film came to service the prosecution's case.'[18]

Douglas identifies yet another way in which the prosecution de-emphasized the crimes against the Jews – not calling Jewish victims to testify before the tribunal. In general, the prosecution downplayed eyewitnesses in favor of documentary evidence, which it considered less vulnerable to attack. Prosecutors called 33 witnesses, just a handful of whom were Jews. More typically, non-Jews testified to atrocities against the Jews. 'The use of non-Jewish witnesses ... was, then, an extension of an evidentiary logic which assumed that proof of extreme crimes became less credible and more impeachable as one moved from perpetrator to bystander to victim,' Douglas argues. He continues:

> [S]uch motives merely reinforced the larger process of displacement, conflation, and assimilation that one finds at work: Just as crimes against humanity were contained within war crimes, so the experiences of Holocaust survivors found restricted expression in the testimony of courtroom proxies.[19]

Given the legal framework in which the case was tried, it is not surprising that the press coverage presented German atrocities as having little to do with Jews. But journalists are not stenographers. Reporters select what to mention and in what order. They pick the words to describe an argument's import, the lawyers' demeanors, the judges' reactions and the audience's response. They provide the context that makes the events intelligible (or not) to the uninformed. Editors then decide whether to publish the story, where to place it in the newspaper, and with what alterations and headline. Other editors might choose to comment on the events in editorials or opinion columns. In other words, journalists make their own judgments about how to depict the events on which they report.

During the Nuremberg trials, the *Times* reporters fully accepted the prosecutors' version of the case, so much so that they departed from standard journalistic practices. They abandoned even the pretense of objectivity or journalistic balance, never referring to 'alleged crimes' or bothering to couch the defendants' guilt in terms of the presumption of innocence. Nor did they challenge the authenticity or reliability of the prosecution's evidence, or suggest an alternative interpretation of witnesses' testimony. Conversely, they freely doubted the testimony of the defendants, their witnesses and the overall thrust of their case. For example, after describing his lawyer's attempt to paint Reich Marshal Hermann Goering as 'a misunderstood leader of a betrayed nation', the *Times* news story said that 'adroit cross-examination' managed 'to bring things into a somewhat better focus'.[20]

If *Times* journalists accepted the prosecution's day-to-day presentation, they also bought its overall strategy. The *Times* signaled through its editorial comments, its descriptions and its placement of stories that it endorsed the placement of aggressive war at the center of the trial. 'We have come to a stage of history,' opined a lead editorial in June 1945, the day after the prosecution's principles were announced, 'where the crime of aggressive war can and must be legally defined'.[21] In fact, when the indictments were presented, the *Times*' only editorial criticism was that the charges

> might have stated in bolder terms the one terrible offense with which these prisoners are charged: planning and making war against humanity. It might have justified more explicitly the absolutely new precedent it seeks to establish – namely, that those who make such a war shall answer for it with their persons.[22]

Once the trial was underway, a lead editorial lauded the proceeding and particularly its willingness to tackle 'the most heinous crime of all, the waging of aggressive war, to which the aforementioned offenses [totalitarianism, the proclamation of a master race, the suppression of civil liberties] were preliminary'.[23] By the time of the verdict, the *Times* editorial page still had not lost its enthusiasm: '[T]he first and foremost [international law principle the verdict establishes] is that the plotting and waging of aggressive war is the "supreme crime," entailing the heaviest punishment', the paper declared.[24]

Editorial writers were not the only ones to consider aggressive war the supreme crime. 'German leaders charged with having incited their nation to aggressive warfare', became the shorthand correspondents employed to describe the trial.[25] They went further; aggressive war was *the* crime against humanity. The American section of the case involved 'conspiracy against the peace, making individuals responsible for that crime against humanity', the *Times* explained.[26] With the end of the American prosecutors' case, Raymond Daniell wrote, all that remained before the defense was to 'complete the story of atrocities the Nazis committed in prosecution of their wars'. Those atrocities were 'enslavement of conquered people and wholesale extermination of Jews and other groups classed as "undesirables".' Still later in the same article, Daniell wrote: 'the crimes which shock the conscience of mankind were all planned and carried out in furtherance of their plan of conquest.'[27]

The *Times* endorsement of the prosecutor's approach can be seen most clearly in its placement of trial stories. In trying the conspiracy count, the Americans introduced evidence supporting all three substantive counts – aggressive war, war crimes and crimes against humanity.[28]

But only during the presentation of conspiracy to wage aggressive war did the *Times* lavish attention on the proceedings. Every news story on the aggressive war conspiracy appeared on the front page (with one important exception, to which I will return), sometimes accompanied by additional inside stories.[29] The placement in the newspaper thus reinforced the primacy of aggressive war, and simultaneously minimized the importance of the extermination of the Jews. Those first few weeks represented the only sustained front-page coverage of the trial, and the *Times*' front-page stories never directly mentioned Jews, except to refer to one defendant, the editor of the anti-Semitic publication *Der Stürmer*, as 'the Jew-baiter, Julius Streicher'.[30] The other references were elliptical. For example, in Kathleen McLaughlin's story announcing the trial's opening, she described defendant Hans Frank as 'governor general of occupied Poland', whose 'barbarism shocked civilization and decimated Polish communities'. She described documents which reviewed the war's 'whole bloody annals', with 'statistics [that] attested to the facts' and 'staggering totals [that] were piled up'. Totals of what, or facts about what, were never mentioned.[31]

McLaughlin's story the next day was just as vague, even though it purported to cover the prosecution's opening statement, in which Justice Robert Jackson, lead counsel, devoted 'an important section to "crimes against the Jews".' Jackson declared: 'The most savage and numerous crimes planned and committed were against the Jews. ... The conspiracy and common plan to exterminate the Jew was so methodically and thoroughly pursued that ... this Nazi aim largely has succeeded.' Michael Marrus concludes that Jackson's statement 'set the tone for future discussion of Nazi anti-Jewish policy by the prosecution'.[32] The statement may have set the tone for discussion of the anti-Jewish policy, but the story about it did not. The story did not quote from that section of Jackson's speech or refer to Jews in any way.[33]

As soon as the prosecution moved from the conspiracy to commit aggressive war to war crimes and crimes against humanity committed in furtherance of that conspiracy – in which the extermination of the Jews at least played a part – the *Times* stories made a nosedive inside. That the *Times*, like other newspapers, would be more interested in the trial at the beginning than the end is not surprising. Indeed, after the initial flurry, only a handful of stories about the proceedings appeared on the front page until the verdicts.[34] (One of the few described French prosecutor Francois de Menthon's opening statement on war crimes and crimes against humanity in the west, which famously never uttered a word about the Jews. Its front-page placement seemed to have less to do with de Menthon's omission of a reference to the Jews, however, than to his call for the death penalty for some defendants – the first such reference by the prosecuting team, according to the story.[35]) But the decision to move trial stories inside the paper did not reflect a gradual loss of interest, with fewer front-page stories appearing over time. As soon as the American prosecution ended its account of aggressive war, so did the *Times*' front-page coverage. The first such inside story, one about slave laborers, explained: that the prosecution had 'turned from proof that Germany had embarked on a deliberate and premeditated program of aggression to evidence of the crimes against humanity committed in the prosecution of those wars'.[36]

According to those inside stories, war crimes and crimes against humanity targeted, in relatively equal measure, all sorts of persecuted peoples. Jews were rarely singled out; instead, they appeared somewhere amidst a litany of sufferers. Consider just one example. A story on 13 December 1945 described the previous day's evidence as focusing on Germany's 'ruthless methods' in 'prisoner-of-war camps and slave labor concentration camps', as well as its 'premeditated mass extermination of "anti-social" elements among the Jews, gypsies, Russians, Ukrainians and Poles'. Further down, it explained that Himmler had ordered 'Jews, Gypsies, Russians, Ukrainians and Poles' to be removed from prisons and sent to concentration camps.[37] When the evidence focused exclusively on what happened to Jews, it was often the last element mentioned in a story. For example, prosecutor William Walsh's presentation of 'evidence of persecution of the Jews at the afternoon session' appeared in the last five paragraphs of a page ten story on 14 December. Another story's lead described the proof presented that Gestapo head Ernst Kaltenbrunner 'had been directly responsible for mass murders, deportations and executions of Allied prisoners'. A bit farther on, the article described Kaltenbrunner's role in 'rounding up slave laborers, exterminating Jews, Poles and Russians and slaughtering prisoners'. Only at the bottom of the story did it become clear that 'topping the list of damning documents' was an affidavit that Kaltenbrunner 'ordered the "liquidation" of two Jewish camps at Landsberg and Mühlendorf' just before US troops reached them.[38] The lead in a February story said that prosecutors had linked three of the defendants 'to the murder of millions of Russians, Poles, Yugoslavs and Czechoslovaks ...' Only later did the story quote the Russian prosecutor as charging defendant Hans Frank with 'the death of "at least 3,000,000 Jews".'[39]

The *Times* stories also overlooked evidence concerning the extermination of the Jews that prosecutors considered critical. For example, the day that American prosecutors established Gestapo chief Kaltenbrunner's role in mass murder, they read into the record an affidavit from Hermann Gräbe, a German construction manager in the Ukraine. Telford Taylor considers Gräbe's affidavit, which described the violent roundup of Jews in Rovno and a mass execution in the Ukraine, 'as horrifying as any in the annals of Nuremberg'.[40] Gräbe's description of a family, including an old woman, a couple, a baby and a 10-year old boy, as they waited to be executed, was so poignant that the British prosecutor used it in his emotional closing.[41] The *Times* ran stories about the trial proceedings in the two days following the reading of Gräbe's affidavit, but neither story mentioned it.[42]

Similarly, the *Times* devoted only a single paragraph to the testimony of Dieter Wislicency, Adolf Eichmann's assistant, who said he helped send more than 600,000 Jews to the gas chambers. Wislicency's time on the stand was 'the single most important testimony for understanding the European-wide evolution of the "Final Solution",' Marrus writes.[43] 'To the judges and the world it was Dieter Wislicency who ... explained the meaning of the phrase "the Final Solution of the Jewish Question",' Robert Conot offers.[44] Not to the readers of the *New York Times*, who got a truncated version. Wislicency, the story explained, had been a 'specialist' in the Jewish question who had been sent to Slovakia, Hungary, and Greece to find a 'solution'.[45] Another important moment came when the prosecution showed a 90-second film shot unofficially in the Warsaw ghetto by a German solider. It showed naked Jewish men and women being dragged through the streets and beaten. The film bore the unambiguous title, *Original 8-millimeter Film of Atrocities Against the Jews*, and prosecutor Walsh described it as 'perhaps one of the most unusual exhibits that will be presented during the trial'.[46] The *Times* mentioned the film in a short item beneath its main trial story, saying only that it was 'taken in a ghetto somewhere in Europe', ' and 'showed women being stripped naked and chased through the streets'.[47] The *Times* completely ignored snapshots, also taken by German soldiers, of Jews jumping from burning ghetto buildings.[48]

The *Times* failure to report the testimony of Jewish victims provides the starkest example of its tendency to downplay the Jewish tragedy even more than the prosecution. The paper never quoted the testimony of a single Jewish witness. Its stories featured the testimony of several non-Jewish victims, including those of Dr Franz Biaha, a 47-year- old Czech physician, who described the visit of six defendants to Dachau where he was imprisoned;[49] Leon van der Essen, a librarian who testified about the German destruction of the famed University of Louvain library;[50] and François Boix, 'a 24-year-old veteran of the French and Spanish Republican armies'.[51] Some of the non-Jewish victims, such as Marie-Claude Valliant-Couturier, who had been in Auschwitz and Ravensbrück, testified to the treatment of Jews. According to the *Times*' account, Valliant-Couturier said that Jewish women were used as human guinea pigs in sterilization experiments, and their babies, if born alive, were drowned in buckets. She recalled awakening one night to the 'horrible cries' of babies hurled alive into the crematorium when the chambers had run out of gas.[52] Some of the non-Jewish victims, such as Maurice Lampe, did not mention Jews. In the *Times* account, Lampe, a Mauthausen prisoner, described how 50 American and Dutch pilots had died while lugging heavy stones from the bottom to the top of a quarry as they were beaten. The *Times* described the camp as holding 'some 500,000 luckless victims of German racial and political ideologies'.[53] When Jewish witnesses took the stand, the *Times* ignored them.[54] (Taylor said there were four;[55] Douglas named three.) 'The importance of these witnesses cannot be gainsaid', Douglas writes, noting that they 'made vivid the constant moral and physical degradation that preceded the killing' and 'presented the trial's most precise testimony about a pure extermination center'.[56] Not a word of their testimony appeared in the *Times*.[57]

This is not to say that the *Times* consistently ignored the destruction of European Jewry. There were many references to 'the blood of 5,700,000 Jews who were systematically exterminated', or to 'the mass murders of Jews in Eastern Europe'.[58] Non-Jewish victims' testimony about what had been done to Jews was included, and perpetrators' testimony, most notably that of Otto Ohlendorf, was sometimes described in detail.[59] Ohlendorf, head of a mobile killing squad that operated from Czernowicz, Poland, to Odessa, testified to his unit's method of rounding up Jews, driving them to a nearby ditch and having a firing squad execute them.[60] The *Times* even ran a page eight story devoted solely to the extermination of the Jews. The unambiguous headline read: 'Trial Data Reveal 6,000,000 Jews Died', although the vague lead somewhat mitigated the effect. 'A story of shame and horror' put before the international tribunal showed that 'after Germans' conquest of the east and west they had sought to create living space for their own people by exterminating all dissident elements of the population and plundering the rest', read the lead.[61]

But more often than not, Jews appeared among a long litany of victims, or at the end of stories that highlighted some other group's tragic plight. Consider one final example. On 26 December 1945 (p. 8), during the trial's Christmas recess, the *Times* printed two photographs, which have since become iconic images of Jewish resistance in the Warsaw ghetto. One was of a small boy in a cap raising his arms in surrender as Nazi soldiers trained their guns on him and on a group of women and children nearby. The other showed adult men and women, their arms raised, marching off, surrounded by soldiers and by burning ghetto buildings. The *Times* headline for the two photographs was: 'Nazi Terrorism in Poland is Brought to Light'. The caption, which provides the only additional text – there is no accompanying article – stated:

> These photographs were among several introduced at the war crimes trials in Nuremberg showing the destruction of Warsaw in the spring of 1943. The pictures were in a report of an SS commander charged with the destruction of the city's Ghetto and the removal of Jews to concentration camps.

The Jewish identity of those depicted was thus not denied, but diminished. An editorial the following day (p. 18) was more oblique. The people in the photograph were described as 'the survivors of the Warsaw ghetto', and 'the starving remnants of a heroic people', but nowhere were they identified as Jews. The editorial at first acknowledged them as individuals: the little boy, 'perhaps 10 years old'; the woman, glancing over her shoulder 'who may have been this boy's mother'; a 'little girl with a pale sweet face'. But then the editorial detracted not just from their Jewish identities, but from their individuality as well. 'These Warsaw pictures' are 'tiny vignettes in a continental horror that came within an ace of engulfing the world', the editorial concluded, as it instructed the reader not to pity the Nuremberg defendants.[62]

That Nuremberg's legal framework did not wholly determine press coverage can be seen by looking at the *Times* handling of another war crime trial. Just before the Nuremberg trials began, the British tried Josef Kramer and 44 'SS henchmen for conspiracy to commit mass murder' at Auschwitz[63] and Bergen-Belsen.[64] Unlike Nuremberg, this trial focused exclusively on mass murder; the atrocities were not adjuncts to some greater crime, they were themselves the crime. In addition, the prosecution relied much more heavily on eyewitness testimony – calling nearly as many witnesses in its three-week presentation as the Nuremberg prosecutors did in four months. Many of them were Jews, as were most of those murdered in Auschwitz, or dragged to Belsen in the war's final days.

Yet Jews figured no more prominently in the *Times* coverage of this trial than they did in its depiction of Nuremberg. The *Times* three front-page stories – coinciding with the opening, sentencing and hanging – never mentioned the word, 'Jew',[65] nor did an editorial applauding the death sentences for 11 defendants.[66] Auschwitz's victims were described as '4,000,000 persons', or 'inmates'. The defendants' actions resulted in 'the deliberate cold-blooded extermination of millions'. Even the inside stories only mentioned Jews in one context – when Jews were testifying.[67] Ada Bimko, '[a] black-haired Polish Jewish woman, her concentration camp number tattoed [*sic*] on her left forearm,' estimated 'with tears streaming down her face,' that '4,000,000 Jews had perished in the [Auschwtitz] murder factory', including her father, mother, brothers, two sisters, husband and 6-year-old son.[68] Dr Sigismund Charles Bendell, a Romanian Jew, testified that 80,000 Jews from the Lodz ghetto were 'killed and burned as fast as they could be pushed through'. He 'omitted no detail: the cries and weeping when the gas chamber doors were forced shut, the noise of fighting inside, the pounding on the walls, the silence after two minutes and the hideous sight when the doors were opened'.[69] The Jewish witnesses quoted refer to Jews incessantly, as if to scream not only look what happened to *me*, but look what happened to *us*.[70] Inevitably, the journalist's narration appeared, stripped of all references to Jews. The defendants' crimes thus were 'participating in a plot with Heinrich Himmler to murder and maltreat Allied nationals through the concentration camp system'.[71] It would take another 15 years for Jewish voices to be heard at the Eichmann trial.

Why did the narrative of aggressive war have such appeal for American journalists while the tale of Jewish annihilation did not? Nuremberg, framed as a trial to judge Germany's top leaders for the crime of waging war, played into three powerful journalistic norms. First, journalists tend to define news as the official actions of top government leaders – a tendency that was even more pronounced in the pre-Vietnam, pre-Watergate era. Prosecutorial decisions about whom to indict neatly coincided with this norm. The prosecution selected defendants not to focus 'responsibility for the mass murder of European Jews', Jeremy Rabkin writes, but to assemble 'the most prominent surviving personages from Hitler's regime'.[72] Those men were 'largely military, political, diplomatic and financial figures', as Allan Ryan points out, whose connection to the 'central apparatus of the Holocaust' was indirect.

For journalists, that meant the trial would have a 'star' cast, even though its luster had dimmed.[73] The defendants were once powerful, still famous Nazi leaders such as Hermann Goering, Rudolf Hess and Joachim von Ribbentrop, no mere functionaries running the Einsatzgruppen in the former Soviet territories, or commanding an extermination center with an unpronounceable Polish name. It also meant that the trial would focus on the decisions they made at the pinnacle of their power. To most journalists, those economic, political, diplomatic and military decisions embodied the very essence of news.[74] So the *Times* top Nuremberg correspondent, Raymond Daniell, who had stopped covering the trial in mid-January, returned to report on Goering's direct testimony. The paper's front-page coverage resumed as well, at least for that day.[75] In an opinion column, Daniell quoted approvingly a witness's comment that Goering was 'the last great figure of the Nazi movement'.[76] Daniell hung around for Hess, Ribbentrop, Keitel and Schact, but let other *Times* reporters and the wire services handle the lesser lights.[77] In a backhanded way, a comment from another correspondent, Drew Middleton, confirms this mindset: 'Much of today's testimony came from the little people of Europe who had their revenge on the hard-faced Germans on trial', he wrote, referring to a Norwegian lawyer, two French army officers and the chief of the Pasteur laboratory in Paris.[78] Middleton, in fact, was so enamored of this phrase he used it again: this time the 'little people of Europe' spoke 'through the mouth' of a French prosecutor.[79]

The trial's focus on aggressive war also tapped into journalists' preference for stories about events that are geographically or emotionally close to their audience, or about topics that readers could relate to. With aggressive war as the trial's centerpiece, the United States became not just a bystander to the defendants' crimes – as it would have been had the focus been on crimes against humanity – the USA itself became a victim. 'As the American prosecutors argued the cases, the top Nazis deserved to be punished for plotting a campaign of aggressive war – a plot so far-reaching that it ultimately dragged a reluctant America into the European conflict', Rabkin explains.[80] This meant that the trial, like the war, would be about American involvement, which also happened to mesh with American correspondents' desire for a narrative of interest to their audience.[81] No similarly potent norms propelled the Jewish genocide to the forefront of journalistic narratives about the Nuremberg trials. As Allan Ryan notes, 'the Jews who had perished in the Holocaust had no sponsor at Nuremberg'. Most Americans were not emotionally close to European Jews, and thus did not easily identify with their travails.[82] Nor were the millions of Jews powerful world figures making what journalists considered to be news; they lacked even a single leading figure, a Pope, as Franklin Roosevelt once lamented.[83]

Finally, and most important, the Nuremberg trial's legal framework fitted journalists' pre-existing understanding of the Second World War and the Jews' role in it. For more than a decade, since the Nazis' rise to power, American journalists had fixated on one overriding story line – America's struggle first to avoid war and then to win it. All sorts of events were assessed in light of that imperative. Domestic political battles, for example, were often explained in terms of whether they would strengthen or weaken the President, and thus would be more or less likely to draw the country into war. The persecution of the Jews also fit into this framework. The Jews were seen as 'scapegoats' in pre-war Germany, persecuted for strategic reasons to abet Nazi power, not because of fundamental anti-Semitic ideology.[84] In the United States they were 'refugees', whose unsolved problems could lure America into a foreign fight.

Once the war started, the press accepted the Allied strategy of downplaying confirmed, credible evidence of the Germans' drive to eradicate European Jewry. The government feared, simultaneously if somewhat contradictorily, that too much attention on the Jews might ratchet up demands for rescue and thus detract from the war effort, or detract from it because Americans would not want to fight a war to save the Jews. The press furthered this strategy through its handling of news about the extermination campaign.[85] Stories about the singular plight of the Jews rarely made the front page. When the Jews were mentioned at all they tended to be grouped with other suffering people – the Poles, the Czechs, the Greeks. The press thus helped to frame the Second World War as an American fight to save all oppressed humanity, encompassing, but only tangentially, the Jews.[86]

Interpretive frameworks, once fixed, tend to change slowly, even as underlying factual circumstances shift. In the first year of peace, journalists were not likely to abandon their wartime perspective. They naturally gravitated toward a narrative that continued to view all events of World War II as arising from Germany's drive for world domination and America's determination to resist it. By contrast, to have focused on the elaborate, time- and resource-consuming campaign to murder Europe's Jews would not only have required a new framework, it would have directly challenged the old one. Journalists would have had to acknowledge that the Germans were so determined to win the war against the Jews that they were willing to suffer losses in their war against America.

Interestingly, all these journalistic imperatives – the focus on the powerful, the fixation on America's role and the framework of wartime issues – can been seen in the *Times* coverage of the *Nazi Concentration Camp* film. Given the film's importance in the collective memory of the Nuremberg trial, one would assume it played an equally climactic part in the *Times* contemporaneous coverage. It did not. For the first seven days of the proceedings, a trial story appeared every day on the paper's front page. The day the film was shown marked the first time such a story was absent. Raymond Daniell's article appeared on page six, suggesting that the atrocities, no matter how horrifyingly evoked, were nowhere near as important as the preceding aggressive war presentations. The story's structure reconfirms that priority. After introducing the film in two paragraphs – 'a one-hour nightmare in motion picture depicting the fear and terror and the nameless horror of the concentration camps' – Daniell immediately segued to a detailed discussion of the annexation of Austria in 1938. Eight long paragraphs later the story returned to the film, which presented 'horror piled on horror and mounting in dreadfulness as it went along', so that it 'was almost more than anyone could bear'. But that was all the article said about the film's content. The film itself, in which Americans (with a few exceptions) were bystanders, not victims, was never described. Instead, the later paragraphs turned to the defendants, those once mighty Nazis brought low, 'whose rapt expressions were illuminated by the dimmed light along the front of the dock'. It was they, the powerful leaders, who continued to make news, not the powerless, barely human figures in the film. Or, as journalist Alex Ross writes, 'the world did not watch to discover the worst acts of the Nazi regime – these, it thought, it already knew – but to pierce the minds of perpetrators'.[87] In his effort to minimize the moment, Daniell also seemingly misread it. While other accounts found the defendants' overcome by their confrontation with evil of their own making, Daniell described the prisoners as 'having less expression than the spectators watching a dull news reel'.[88] Daniell, it seems, was impatient to get back to the Anschluss.

The film gives rise to one final point. The language of the narration, whose meaning Douglas parses so effectively, resembles descriptions of camp liberations in the *Times*' news stories. Majdanek's inmates were '1,500,000 persons from nearly every country in Europe'. In Buchenwald, they were 'non-descript prisoners'. Dachau held 'Russians,

Poles, Frenchmen, Czechs and Austrians'.[89] In other words, those imprisoned in concentration and extermination camps were described as just about anything but Jews. The similarity to the *Nazi Concentration Camp* narration is striking, but not coincidental. Prosecutors took the narration directly from the reports of the military photographers who had filmed the camps.[90] In fact, the film's description of inmates at the Ohrdurf concentration camp that Douglas singles out appeared word-for-word in a *New York Times* story about the camp's liberation. The *Times* reported that those killed included 'Poles, Czechs, Russians, Belgians, Frenchmen, German Jews and German political prisoners'.[91] The narration therefore reflected not just a legal strategy, but a world-view. Military photographers, journalists, even Nuremberg prosecutors tended not to recognize, or at least to acknowledge, the Jews amidst the 'non-descript' prisoners,' the citizens of 'nearly every country in Europe'. The American prosecutors' Nuremberg strategy, therefore, may have been as much a byproduct and perpetuator of this perspective as a creator of it.[92]

Because the Jews were not noticed does not mean they were not there – in Buchenwald, in Dachau, in Majdanek, in Belsen, in Auschwitz, and at Nuremberg. Plenty of evidence could be found among the reams of court documents to tell what happened to the Jews, as Marrus well documents. But neither the prosecutors who presented the case, nor the journalists who summarized it in daily dispatches, constructed a meaningful narrative from those pieces.[93] As a result, the American public's understanding of German crimes in the immediate post-war period did not recognize the horror of the Jewish genocide. The press thus contributed to a form of Holocaust denial, not a denial of what happened, but a denial of its meaning and significance, that, for purposes of collective memory, is the same thing.

NOTES

1. Carlos S. Nino, *Radical Evil on Trial* (New Haven, CT: Yale University Press, 1996), p. 131, likens such trials to Bruce Ackerman's constitutional moments: 'The drama of a trial, with the victims and perpetrators under the public light, with accusations and defenses, with witnesses from all social sectors, and with the terrifying prospect of punishment, inevitably attracts great public attention and may even provoke "dummy" trials in the streets or around dinner tables.'
2. Allan A. Ryan Jr. cogently explains how the Nuremberg trial came to be about 'Germany's 12-year policy of international aggression,' and 'not primarily about the Holocaust'.
3. Lawrence Douglas, *The Memory of Judgment: Making Law and History in the Trials of the Holocaust* (New Haven and London: Yale University Press, 2001), pp. 66, 89. See also Mark Osiel, *Mass Atrocity, Collective Memory and the Law* (New Brunswick, NJ: Transaction Publishers, 1997), p. 97, who argues that courts should 'admit a wider range of evidence and argument than are often cognizable within strictly legal terms', to do justice to the historical records. 'In fact, it borders on the obscene to resolve so historiographically momentous and

morally weighty a question as "the cause of the Holocaust" – for purposes of collective memory – on the basis of so narrow and peculiarly professional a preoccupation as the terms of a treaty's jurisdictional provision.'

4. 'Nuremberg Trials and the Holocaust', *Yad Vashem Studies*, Vol. 26 (1998), pp. 5–41, quote from p. 6.

5. In *Judgment on Nuremberg* (Chapel Hill, NC: University of North Carolina Press, 1970), William J. Bosch assesses the reaction of various American constituencies, including the public and the press, to the trial. His comprehensive analysis of the coverage of 31 newspapers, based on editorials and opinion columns, however, focuses primarily on whether the papers approved or disapproved of the trial. He does not analyze the day-to-day coverage, nor does he address the specific issue of how either the prosecution or the press presented the Holocaust.

6. *The Anatomy of the Nuremberg Trials: A Personal Memoir* (New York: Alfred A. Knopf, 1992), p. 209. See also Bosch, *Judgment on Nuremberg*, p. 88: 'The average American gains his knowledge about the facts and personalities of the war-crime trials from the opinion media readily accessible to him – the daily newspaper, the columnists' feature articles, and popular magazines.' Popular magazine articles, such as those by Janet Flanner and Rebecca West in the *New Yorker*, were influential, though both authors concentrated mostly on the trial's atmospherics rather than on the substance of either the prosecution's or defense's presentations.

7. My concern here is solely with the American press. Press coverage in other Allied countries was likely to have been quite different. Nine months into the trial, the *Times* noted that 'only the British correspondents (perhaps operating on the cricket psychology that the longer a thing lasts, the better it is) continued to file detailed daily accounts.' 21 July 1946, p. 2E. One of the only studies to take a systematic look at war crimes trials' coverage found a marked difference between the German and the Israeli press (or, in the case of Nuremberg, the Jewish press in prestatehood Palestine). Akiba Cohen, Tamar Zemach-Marom, Jurgen Wilke and Birgit Schenk, *The Holocaust and the Press: Nazi War Crimes Trials in Germany and Israel*, (Creskill, NJ: Hampton Press Inc., 2002).

8. Even the *Times* eventually lost heart. Six months into the trial, it sent its reporters elsewhere and relied on Associated Press and United Press wire service stories, although those continued to appear almost every day.

9. Just a month and a half into the trial, the *Times* correspondent covering it bemoaned the fact that 'the trial is getting scant attention in the American press outside the big metropolitan dailies in the East.' *New York Times*, 6 January 1946, p. 5E. Six months later, the *Times* noted that American press coverage had been 'reduced to news agency representatives and occasional visitors.' 21 July 1946, p. 1E. The correspondents left standing joked that they were the last victims of the Nuremberg prosecution. Bosch, *Judgment on Nuremberg*, p. 95. See also Taylor, *Anatomy of the Nuremberg Trials*, p. 221.

10. A quarter of the *Times* weekday readers and half of its Sunday readers were outside the New York area. Matthew Josephson, 'Typewriter Statesman', *Saturday Evening Post*, 216:5, 29 July 1944, p. 9. In addition, its syndicate sent articles from the *Times* to 525 newspapers, including such important ones as the *Detroit Free Press*, *Chicago Tribune*, the *Denver Post*, the *Los Angeles Times* and the *San Francisco Chronicle*. F. E. Meinholtz to James, no date, mid-1943, Edwin L. James File, Raymond Daniell Folder, New York Times Company Archives.

11. *The Disappearing Daily: Chapters in American Newspaper Evolution* (New York: Alfred A. Knopf, 1944), p. 78. Washington correspondents confirmed that judgment in a 1944 survey, concluding by more than five to one that the *Times* was the nation's most reliable and comprehensive newspaper. Deborah Lipstadt, *Beyond Belief: The American Press and the Coming of the Holocaust 1933–1945* (New York: The Free Press, 1986), p. 171.

12. Journalists were also still reeling from their encounters with the newly liberated concentration camps, which Barbie Zelizer, *Remembering to Forget: Holocaust Memory Through the Camera's Eye* (Chicago: University of Chicago Press, 1998), pp. 65–8, nicely summarizes.

13. The Nuremberg trials ultimately proved less satisfying than hoped, as they stretched on over ten months. When Rebecca West arrived there for the *New Yorker* magazine in August 1946, she found the courtroom to be 'a citadel of boredom'. *New Yorker*, 7 September 1946, pp. 34–46, quote from p. 34. 'Journalists ordinarily prefer short-term events, and when possible those that begin and end within the publication cycle of the medium (day, week, month, etc.)', Cohen, Zemach-Marom, Wilke and Schenk, *The Holocaust and the Press*, pp. 142-3.

14. Bosch, *Judgment on Nuremberg*, p. 94, concludes that it was the largest group to cover one

event, although he sets the figure at 160 journalists. Others have relied on a higher number of between 240 and 250, based on the number of seats reserved for the press in the courtroom. Robert E. Conot, *Justice at Nuremberg* (New York: Harper & Row Publishers, 1983), p. 103, and Douglas, *The Memory of Judgment*, p. 13. Cohen, Zemach-Marom, Wilke, and Schenk's estimate of about 250 journalists covering the trial seems the most reliable, given their country-by-country breakdown of the press presence: *The Holocaust and the Press*, p. 12.
15. They included Kathleen McLaughlin, one of the few female war correspondents; Drew Middleton, a former war correspondent who would one day head the *Times*'s London bureau; and Sidney Gruson, who became a top *Times* executive after a long career as a foreign correspondent.
16. My summary of the legal issues is based upon Douglas's excellent analysis in *The Memory of Judgment*.
17. Ibid., pp. 55-6.
18. Ibid., pp. 62-4.
19. Ibid., pp. 78-9.
20. 9 March 1946, p. 4.
21. 8 June 1945, p. 18.
22. 19 October 1945, p. 22.
23. 25 November 1945, p. 8E.
24. 1 October 1946, p. 22.
25. 20 November 1945, p. 6.
26. 25 November 1945, p. 1E.
27. 6 January 1946, p. 5.
28. As others have pointed out, opening with consideration of the conspiracy charge, which encompassed elements of the other counts, made the latter stages of the trial redundant, and partially accounts for the press's lack of lasting interest in the proceedings.
29. 22 November 1945, pp. 1, 2, 3; 23 November 1945, p. 1; 24 November 1945, p. 1; 27 November 1945, p. 1; 28 November 1945, pp. 1, 15; 29 November 1945, p. 1, 10; 1 December 1945, p. 1, 7; 2 December 1945, p. 1; 5 December 1945, p. 1; 6 December 1945, p.1. On the days not listed, there were no trials' stories at all, except on Monday, 26 November when a page-three story anticipated that day's trial events after a weekend break.
30. There were also variations on the theme: 'Julius Streicher, leading anti-Semite' (25 November 1945, p. 1E), or 'Streicher, the dim-witted and fanatical Jew-baiter' (1 December 1945, p. 22), or 'Streicher, the sadistic, Jew-baiting Gauleiter of Franconia' (11 January 1946, p. 6). Interestingly, this repeated refrain made it seem as if Streicher was *the* anti-Semite among the group.
31. 21 November, 1945, p. 1.
32. 'The Holocaust at Nuremberg,' p. 14.
33. 22 November 1945, p. 2.
34. Even subsequent stories about the British presentation of the aggressive war count appeared inside the paper, (January 5, 1946, p. 6, 9 January 1946, p. 15, 10 January 1946, p. 12, 16 January 1946, p. 6, 17 January 1946, p. 14), including some that might have seemed to be of particular interest to Americans, such as one on Grand Admiral Doenitz's order that German submarines destroy Allied crews as well as Allied ships (15 January 1946, p. 11) and another that documented Germans' harsh treatment of American prisoners of war (31 January 1946, p. 9.) Three months into the trial, a *Times* editorial almost apologetically noted: 'When a running story in a newspaper begins to be more of the same, and doesn't surprise people any more, it is taken off the front page and put inside somewhere. This practice follows a sort of natural law of journalism. Just now it gives the Nuremberg trials a back seat.' (21 February 1946, p. 20.) The truth is that the *Times* had been giving the trial a back seat since the American presentation on aggressive war had ended, more than two months earlier.
35. 18 January 1946, p.1. The other front-page stories described the sinking of the *Athenia* liner, with 28 Americans aboard, during the first week of war (January 16, 1946); a secret agreement between Germany and Russia (21 March 1946); Hans Frank's confession (19 April 1946); and Justice Jackson's summation (27 July 1946).
36. 12 December 1945, p. 4.
37. 13 December 1945, p. 12.
38. 3 January 1946, p. 6.

39. 16 February 1946, p. 6.
40. Taylor, *Anatomy of the Nuremberg Trials*, p. 244.
41. Douglas, *Memory of Judgment*, pp. 92-3.
42. 3 January 1946, p. 3 and 4 January 1946, p. 6.
43. 'The Holocaust at Nuremberg,' p. 21.
44. Robert E. Conot, *Justice at Nuremberg* (New York: Harper & Row, 1983, p. 257.
45. 4 January 1946, p. 6.
46. Douglas, *Memory of Judgment*, p. 68. Marrus, 'The Holocaust at Nuremberg,' p. 19, also considers the film and snapshots an example of 'drama and intensity' that 'focused attention on Jews'.
47. 14 December 1945, p. 10.
48. The snapshots and film made more of an impression on Janet Flanner, who wrote about the trial periodically for the *New Yorker* magazine. She considered the film 'special', providing a 'clear view of naked Jews, male and female, moving with a floating, unearthly slowness and a nightmare-like dignity among the clubs and kicks of the laughing German soldiers.'
49. 14 January 1946, p. 6.
50. 5 February 1946, p. 10.
51. 29 January 1946, p. 8.
52. Ibid.
53. 26 January 1946, p.8.
54. The *Times* did record the testimony of Jacob Grigoriev, who told of the murder of his wife, two of his three sons and the rest of his village, but he is described only as a 'Russian peasant'. 27 February 1946, p. 14.
55. Taylor, *Anatomy of Nuremberg*, p. 317.
56. Douglas, *Memory of Judgment*, p. 78.
57. The *Times*'s lack of interest in survivors' testimony may seem odd, particularly in light of current journalistic preferences for emotional, human stories over factual documentation, as Tim Cole discusses in 'The Holocaust and its (re)telling'. However, the personal anecdote was not a common narrative technique in mid-century journalism, and survivors' stories are missing from most post-liberation accounts. In August 1945, for example, the *Times* ran an unusually long front-page story on conditions among the Jews in various European countries. The entire story quoted only three Jewish survivors, each of whom held a quasi-official position, and included not a single personal narrative (26 August 26, 1945, p. 1).
58. 19 October 1945, p. 1 and 11 January 1946, p. 6.
59. Marrus, 'The Holocaust at Nuremberg', p. 21, considers Ohlendorf 'a very important witness'.
60. 4 January 1946, p. 6.
61. 15 December 1945, p. 8.
62. The *Times* editorial page had a tortured history commenting on the Warsaw ghetto uprising. It never editorialized as the ghetto burned, although the paper's news pages ran numerous stories about the battle. When, six months later, the *Times* ran an editorial on the uprising, it never mentioned that the fighters were Jews (28 October 1943, p. 22). After being severely criticized for this omission by Jewish groups, the first anniversary editorial referred to 'Jewish martyrs' (21 April 1944, p. 18).
63. The *Times* stories consistently refer to the camp by its Polish name, Oswiecim, but I have chosen to use the more familiar German name.
64. Taylor, *Anatomy of the Nuremberg Trials*, p. 271, notes that the trial 'got a very bad press' because of the defense mounted by the mostly British counsel. The press criticism, which was muted in the *Times* at any rate (see 12 October 1945, p. 10 and 9 November 1945, p. 6), does not undermine the Kramer trial's usefulness as a basis of comparison with Nuremberg. Whatever problems might have arisen during the defense would not have affected coverage of the prosecution, with which I am primarily concerned.
65. 18 September 1945, p. 1, 18 November 1945, p. 1 and 15 December 1945, p. 1.
66. 19 November 1945, p. 20.
67. See 19 September 1945, p. 21, 20 September 1945, p. 5, 22 September 1945, p. 5, 23 September 1945, p. 26, 25 September 1945, p. 12, 27 September 1945, p. 12, 28 September 1945, p. 8, 30 September 1945, p. 39, 2 October 1945, p. 3, 6 October 1945, p. 7, 7 October 1945, p. 9, 9 October 1945, p. 3, 10 October 1945, p. 8, 11 October 1945, p. 4, 16 October 1945, p. 6, 21

October 1945, p. 11, 23 October 1945, p. 4, 4 November 1945, p. 29, 14 November 1945, p. 2, 17 November 1945, p. 7, and 9 December 1945, p. 26.
68. At that point, the article actually stated that her family died upon arriving in Belsen, but I assume that is the reporter's mistake. The story later paraphrased Bimko's testimony about arriving at Auschwitz with her family and other Jews from her town in Poland. She then said of the 5,000 Jews who arrived at the camp that 500 were admitted, while the rest, including every member of her family except herself, were taken to the gas chambers. That version is more consistent with the operations of the two camps, because Belsen was not an extermination center where inmates were typically murdered on arrival. 22 September 1945, p. 5.
69. 2 October 1945, p. 3.
70. Even here, in quoting these witnesses, the unnamed reporter or reporters – none of the stories bears a byline – seemed uncomfortable, particularly with their emotionalism: one woman's 'answers came in a torrent of emotional descriptions' (23 September 1945, p. 26); another 'burst into tears and had to be taken from the courtroom' (25 September 1945, p. 12). The reporter's evident distaste foreshadows Hannah Arendt's expectation of 'conventional, rational behavior' from the Jewish witnesses during the Eichmann trial. Pnina Lahav, 'The Eichmann Trial, the Jewish Question, and the American-Jewish Intelligentsia', *Boston University Law Review*, 72, pp. 555, 573.
71. 14 November 1945, p. 2.
72. Jeremy Rabkin, 'Nuremberg Misremembered', *SAIS Review*, Vol. 19, No. 2 (1999), pp. 81-96, quote from p. 82.
73. Consider Kathleen McLaughlin's description of the key defendants the day the trial began: Goering was 'pompous, the exhibitionist, shorn of his medals and glitter'; Hess, 'once the glamour boy of the National Socialist regime and now a self-professed psychiatric case'; and von Ribbentrop: 'a wan shadow of the blustering champagne salesman turned diplomat'. (21 November 1945, p. 1.)
74. Personal obsessions as well as professional norms may also have played a role. Many of the *Times* correspondents covering the trial – Daniell, Long, Middleton – had been journalists during the events that were part of Nuremberg's legal and historical record. The thousands of captured German documents revealed the behind-the-scenes stories – why the Munich peace talks failed, how the Anschluss was engineered – that reporters had only hinted at in their earlier news reports. At Nuremberg, they had the inside scoop, and they were determined to let their readers know it. This seemed to produce a disproportionate fascination with the minutiae of German war plans.
75. 14 March 1946.
76. 24 March 1946, p. 6E.
77. Interestingly, the murder of the Jews seemed to figure more prominently in *Times* reports on the defense than it did those on the prosecution – from Goering's pathetic argument that he condemned Kristallnacht because of the waste of material, to Rudolf Höss's chilling and damning testimony about his efficient operation of Auschwitz (15 March 1946, p. 11, and 5 March 1945, p. 5). .It is as if defendants, aware of the monstrousness of their crimes against the Jews, felt obliged to defend against an allegation the prosecution had never clearly raised. See also March 8, 1946, p. 3, March 9, 1946, p. 4, 22 March 1946, p. 7, 12 April 1946, p. 8, 13 April 1946, p. 10, 14 April 1946, p. 23, 16 April 1946, p. 10, 30 April 1946, p. 4, and 7 May 1946, p. 9.
78. 30 January 1946, p. 13.
79. 1 February 1946, p. 7.
80. *SAIS Review*, pp. 85-6.
81. In comparing coverage of the Nuremberg trial by the German press and the Jewish press in pre-state Palestine, Israeli and German scholars found a similar preference for a theme to which the audience could relate:. '[T]he Jewish press in Palestine already gave more weight to the murder of Jews than did the German press, which instead featured the preparation for and the waging of war as they appeared in the indictments,' they concluded. Cohen, Zemach-Marom, Wilke and Schenk, *The Holocaust and the Press*, p. 138.
82. An obvious exception was the American-Jewish community. It would therefore be interesting to explore the American-Jewish press's coverage of Nuremberg. It is also interesting to ponder whether sympathy for European Jews could have been established through extended personal narratives, or even shorter ones. *The New York Times's* famous 'portraits' of September 11 victims come to mind.

83. Henry L. Feingold, *Bearing Witness: How America and Its Jews Responded to the Holocaust* (Syracuse, NY: Syracuse University Press, 1995), p. 249.
84. See Lipstadt, *Beyond Belief*, pp. 40–62.
85. For a detailed discussion of the interplay between US government policy and newspaper reporting with regard to the Jews, see pp. 236–264 and chapters X and XI of my book, *Buried by The Times: The Holocaust and America's Most Important Newspaper*. (New York: Cambridge University Press, 2005).
86. For a fuller discussion, see Lipstadt, *Beyond Belief*, and Laurel Leff, 'When the Facts Didn't Speak for Themselves: The Holocaust in the *New York Times*, 1939–1945', *Harvard International Journal of Press/Politics*, Vol. 5, No. 2, (2000), pp. 52–72.
87. *New York Times*, 12 November 1995, part 2, p. 37.
88. 30 November 1945, p. 6. His *Times* colleague, Anne O'Hare McCormick, wrote in an opinion column the following day that 'the defendants showed more emotion than at any other session of the trial', describing Ribbentrop as shuddering and wiping his eyes, Doenitz turning white, Von Papen unable even to look at the screen (1 December 1945, p. 22). Daniell ended up taking back his statement about the defendants' unemotional response. In a column he wrote for the Sunday editorial page, he noted that 'psychologists who watched the defendants' concluded that the prisoners, except for Schacht, 'were visibly moved' (2 December 1945, p. E3).
89. 30 August 1944, p. 1, 18 April 1945, p. 1 and 1 May 1945, p. 1.
90. Taylor, *Anatomy of the Nuremberg Trials*, p. 186.
91. 9 April 1945, p. 5. This suggests that the military photographers and journalists, and subsequently prosecutors, relied upon some sort of written description supplied by the military authorities.
92. An interesting question, beyond the scope of this chapter, is the extent to which the interpretive frameworks that arose during the war affected the American prosecution's Nuremberg strategy. As Rabkin, in the *SAIS Review*, p. 91, contends: 'The moral limitations of the trials reflected their dominant purpose, which was the vindication of Allied war aims. Putting an end to Nazi genocide was not a distinct war aim or even a prominent theme of Allied war propaganda, so it did not become a central theme of the postwar trials.' A related issue is the extent to which American prosecutors, cognizant of these sentiments, especially among the American public, shaped their trial strategy to conform to them – what in modern parlance might be called spin. Bosch, *Judgment on Nuremberg*, pp. 116, 33, notes how neatly Nuremberg's guiding principles fitted American ideals: '[A] sophisticated judgment might be made that the administration leaders, consciously or unconsciously, were forced to operate within a framework of possibilities allowed by and acceptable to the American public.' Prosecutors seemed to react to the press during the trial. Conot, *Justice at Nuremberg*, p. 149, records them as putting on certain witnesses to quell press criticism, mostly about the trial's slow pace. Taylor, *Anatomy of the Nuremberg Trials*, pp. 220, 53–5, 172, 197, 261, 305, 220–21, however, insists that although 'the press might and did complain of the lack of drama', the case 'was being tried to the judges, not the press'. He further writes: 'I never heard Jackson mention any press reaction, and I do not believe that the newspapers had much effect on the conduct of the trial.' At other points, however, he takes note of press response, particularly the fact that the British prosecution received more favorable notices than the American. Justice Jackson himself felt obligated to write an article for the *Times* magazine responding to criticism that had appeared in the *Atlantic Monthly*. See the *New York Times Magazine*, 16 June 1946, p. 12.
93. Robert Conot's *Justice at Nuremberg* offers an example of how a powerful narrative of the Nuremberg trials can be constructed with the Final Solution as its center.

9

Jewish Identity, the International Tribunal at Nuremberg and the Eichmann Trial

ALLAN A. RYAN, JR.

The issue of Jewish identification in the trial of the major Nazi war criminals at the International Military Tribunal (IMT) at Nuremberg in 1945 and in the trial of Adolf Eichmann in Israel in 1961 raises an intriguing comparison, although I think it's a bit confining to think of it solely in those terms. The contrast between the two trials is more noticeable if we approach it as a matter of genocide awareness, or of Holocaust awareness, as well as of Jewish identification. I say this because, contrary to the impression some people might have today, Nuremberg was not primarily about the Holocaust. It was primarily about the war – and specifically about Germany's 12-year policy of international aggression that pulverized Europe and was only defeated by a long and costly counter-campaign by the Allies.

It was the Allies' idea – although, really, United States Chief Prosecutor Robert Jackson's idea – to cast the charges as a conspiracy to violate international law. The conspiracy, as Jackson saw it, took two forms: Germany's violation of treaties with its neighbors, and its conduct of a war of aggression apart from treaty violations. This was the basis of what the Nuremberg charter called the 'crime against peace'.

It had nothing to do with the Holocaust, because, as we should remember, the Holocaust was chiefly a social offensive conducted behind the front lines. At the risk of oversimplification, it's useful to recall that the execution of the Holocaust depended on concealment, denial, and the complexity of a bureaucracy run not by the military, but by the SS and civilian ministries. Of course, the bureaucracy needed to be coordinated with the military – in the Einsatzgruppen operations, for example. The military itself was deeply involved in crimes in occupied areas. But as Raul Hilberg laid out in such compelling detail decades ago,[1] the Holocaust needed its own vast machinery, apart from, and sometimes at the expense of, what the Wehrmacht needed to fight the war.

Just as the Allies were not motivated to enter the war to save the Jews of Europe, so they were not, after the war, motivated to create a judicial forum to redress the crimes against them. As early as the Moscow declaration of 1943, the Allies, well aware by then of the crimes against the Jews, warned only that 'major criminals whose offenses have no particular geographic location' would be punished by a 'joint decision of the Allies'.[2] It is not likely that by 'offenses' they had in mind the Einsatzgruppen, the ghettoes or the concentration and death camps. They had in mind the conquest of Europe directed by Hitler and the German General Staff.

Even as late as June 7 1945, just four months before he stood to deliver the opening argument at Nuremberg, Robert Jackson reported to President Truman on the outlines of the case he would be putting together that summer. What is remarkable about this report is that Jackson, although repeatedly referring to the barbarities, atrocities and crimes committed by the Nazis, never referred specifically to the persecution and murder of the Jews of Europe. The core of his case against the Nazis, he said, would be to focus on two things: what they did in Germany and what they did internationally. Internally, he said, the Nazis were

> a band of brigands, set on subverting within Germany every vestige of a rule of law which would entitle an aggregation of people to be looked upon collectively as a member of the family of nations. Our people were outraged by the oppressions, the cruelest forms of torture, the large-scale murder, and the wholesale confiscation of property which initiated the Nazi regime within Germany. They witnessed persecution of the greatest enormity on religious, political and racial grounds, the breakdown of trade unions, and the liquidation of all religious and moral influences.[3]

Internationally, it was clearly the course of aggression that concerned Jackson. 'They bribed, debased, and incited to treason the citizens and subjects of other nations,' he said.

> They ignored the commonest obligations of one state respecting the internal affairs of another. They lightly made and promptly

broke international engagements as part of their settled policy to deceive, corrupt and overwhelm ... Then, in consummation of their plan, the Nazis swooped down upon the nations they had deceived and ruthlessly conquered them. They flagrantly violated the obligations which states, including their own, have undertaken by convention or tradition as a part of the rules of land warfare, and of the law of the sea. They wantonly destroyed cities like Rotterdam for no military purpose. They wiped out whole populations, as at Lidice, where no military purposes were to be served. They confiscated the property of the Poles and gave it to party members. They transported in labor battalions great sectors of the civilian populations of the conquered countries. They refused the ordinary protections of law to the populations which they enslaved.[4]

Jackson was not unaware of, or insensitive to, the crimes against the Jews. Many of the Nazi actions he laid out in those two paragraphs were integral to the Holocaust. But he secularized them. He gave 'persecution of the greatest enormity on religious, political and racial grounds' equal billing with hostility to trade unions. He refers to Rotterdam without mentioning the Jews of Holland, who, says Hilberg, 'were destroyed with a thoroughness comparable to the relentless uprooting process which had struck the Jews in the Reich itself'[5] – 140,000 Jews, of whom three-fourths were murdered.[6] He singled out the massacre of 199 Czech men at Lidice in 1942, but not – speaking of ruthless deception – Theresienstadt. He refers to the Jews, but he generalizes them – one might say he disguises them – as 'Poles', 'civilian populations,' and 'citizens and subjects'.

This aversion to acknowledging the Jewishness of the Holocaust was not unusual in post-war America; indeed, it was typical of it. I have outlined elsewhere the consequences it had in the Displaced Persons Act.[7] David Wyman has analyzed this aversion thoroughly,[8] therefore I will not plow that territory here. I will, however, look at how both the awareness of the Holocaust and the secularization of it were manifested in the trial itself.

Clearly, the centerpiece of the crimes defined by the Charter of the Tribunal was the crime against peace, or aggressive war. The defendants were also charged with war crimes: mistreatment of prisoners of war, execution of captured soldiers, plunder of private property and a host of other crimes that had been recognized in international law for centuries.

But what the Nazis had done to the Jews were not war crimes, because in order to have war crimes, you must first have a war. The Holocaust began before there was any war in Europe, and even after 1939 it was largely removed from the armed conflict where the laws of war could reach. In fact, international law before Nuremberg had no real way of dealing with what had been done, yet Jackson and the Allied prosecutors could not overlook the crimes against the Jews. Therefore they plucked a phrase from the shambles of war crimes prosecutions after World War I: crimes against humanity, rather vaguely defined as inhumane acts against civilians and persecutions on political, racial or religious grounds.

The prosecutors thus put the destruction of the Jews of Europe side by side with the Nazis' mistreatment of political opponents and with crimes committed against other innocent 'populations'. The very detailed indictment included a description of 'genocide', which it defined as 'the extermination of racial and national groups', listing the victims of genocide as 'particularly Jews, Poles, and Gypsies and others'.[9] The prominence of Gypsies in the indictment is curious, because the prosecutors showed little actual interest in the persecution of the Roma (the name now preferred) and there were few references in the trial itself to crimes against them.[10]

The selection of the defendants, likewise, did not unduly focus attention on the Holocaust. Most of the 22 men in the dock were senior officials. They were largely military, political, diplomatic and financial figures: only Ernst Kaltenbrunner, head of the Reichssicherheitshauptamt, the central department of the SS, was intimately involved in the central apparatus of the Holocaust, athough three or four others had regional responsibilities as gauleiters (district administrators) or other civil officials in occupied areas; Goering, Rosenberg and Streicher also played roles.

There was evidence of the Holocaust in the trial itself, particularly film footage taken at the liberation of death camps by British and American troops, although some have suggested that this ghastly evidence was introduced chiefly to recapture the world's fading interest in the trial. And Jackson, in his closing argument, did pause to single out the Holocaust, briefly but powerfully: 'The Nazi movement will be of evil memory in history because of its persecution of the Jews, the most far-flung and terrible racial persecution of all time.'

The focus on the Holocaust was also sharpened, again briefly, in the judgment, handed down on October 1, 1946, after nearly ten months of trial and several weeks' deliberation. The judges were unequivocal: 'The persecution of the Jews at the hands of the Nazi Government has been proved in the greatest detail before this Tribunal,' they said. 'It is a record of consistent and systematic inhumanity on the greatest scale.'[11] Still, the judges wrote 84 pages discussing the evidence under the various charges, and of these pages the number allocated to the discussion of the persecution of the Jews was five: a balance necessarily influenced, of course, by the emphases of the Charter, the indictment and the evidence, none of which placed the Holocaust at center stage.

I'm not suggesting that Jackson, or the judges, denigrated the seriousness of the genocide against the Jews, but clearly they saw it as something to be placed in the larger context of Nazi lawlessness. That is not an indefensible judgment by any means. Today, when we look back and say the Holocaust *was* the context of Nazi lawlessness, it is important to remember that it was seen at the time as a crime that was subsumed, with all the others, in Germany's march across Europe, the crime of conspiracy against peace itself. The prosecutors did not see themselves as especially representing European Jewry, but rather the entire civilized world, or at least the Euro-American civilized world – a world they saw, correctly, as threatened to its very foundations by the Third Reich.

It is also true, I think, that each of the four Allies wanted to shape the court's agenda in ways that reflected the damage the Nazis had inflicted on that country; neither the USA nor Britain had lost Jews to the Holocaust; the Soviet Union had, of course, but it consistently downplayed the Jewish identity of those victims at Nuremberg and for decades afterwards. The deportations of Jews from France was accomplished with much help from French collaborators, a fact that the post-war government was not exactly eager to highlight. In short, the Jews who had perished in the Holocaust had no sponsor at Nuremberg. While the four Allies were quite ready to consign the Holocaust to the long list of Nazi crimes, it served no particular interest of any nation to push for its inclusion high on the list.

Because one focus of this book is memory and denial, I would like to call attention briefly to an important document that is sometimes overlooked: Justice Jackson's final report to President Truman on October 7 1946, in which he summarizes the accomplishments of the IMT. He notes, quite correctly, that the trial established the principle that aggressive war and massive political persecution on racial, religious or political grounds are crimes under international law, and that it provided a fair judicial model that could be used in future international trials – although, as we know, it would be nearly half a century before that actually happened. But it is intriguing that Jackson thought it appropriate to include the following as one of the six accomplishments of the trial:

> We have documented from German sources the Nazi aggressions, persecutions and atrocities with such authenticity and in such detail that there can be no responsible denial of these crimes in the future and no tradition of martyrdom of the Nazi leaders can arise among informed people.[12]

Was Jackson foreseeing a day when revisionism would raise its ugly head? I think he was. He was perhaps thinking more of German nationalism than of anti-Semitism as such, but I think he would not have been surprised to learn that 55 years after he wrote those words, the branch of anti-Semitism known as revisionism is persistent enough to warrant our vigilance.

The contrast of the Eichmann trial could hardly be more striking. That trial was all about Jewish identity: not only Holocaust awareness, but the identity of Jews as a people and as a state. Eichmann, the head of the Jewish Affairs section of the Gestapo and a man whose name had surfaced more than once in the testimony at Nuremberg, was captured in Argentina by Israeli agents in 1960 and hustled to Jerusalem, where he went on trial before three Israeli judges in 1961. The investigation and preparation of the case, and the trial itself, were carried out entirely by the state of Israel under the supervision of its Attorney-General, Gideon Hausner, who was the lead trial counsel. As Hausner later wrote:

> From the moment Prime Minister David Ben-Gurion announced Eichmann's capture, Israel itself was on trial. The whole world seemed to be watching to see how we acquitted ourselves of the task we had undertaken ... In Israel people were anxious that we should begin with the trial as early as possible. It was too much of a nervous strain for the public to live very long in expectation of it.[13]

In fact, Hausner acknowledged that as he prepared the case against Eichmann, the post-war generation of Israelis was very much on his mind. '[W]e needed more than a conviction,' he said:

> [W]e needed a living record of a gigantic human and national disaster ... I wanted our people at home to know as many of the facts of the great disaster as could be legitimately conveyed through these proceedings. It was imperative for the stability of our youth that they should learn the full truth of what had happened, for only through knowledge could understanding and reconciliation be achieved. Our younger generation, absorbed as it was in the building and guarding

of the new state, had far too little insight into events which ought to be a pivotal point in its education. The teen-agers of Israel, most of them born into statehood or during the struggle for it, had no real knowledge, and therefore no appreciation, of the way in which their own flesh and blood had perished. There was here a breach between the generations, a possible source of an abhorrence of the nation's yesterday. This could be removed only by factual enlightenment.[14]

Far from placing the genocide of the Jewish people in the context of a dozen years of Nazi lawlessness, then, the trial of Eichmann *was* the trial of the Holocaust.

The district court of Jerusalem acknowledged this in the opening words of its judgment:. '[T]he counts of the indictment encompass the catastrophe which befell the Jewish people during that period – a story of bloodshed and suffering which will be remembered to the end of time.' The court went on: 'This is not the first time that the Holocaust has been discussed in court proceedings,' it said, referring to the IMT. '[B]ut this time it has occupied the central place in the Court proceedings, and it is this fact which has distinguished this trial from those which preceded it.'[15]

But the most powerful statement of Jewish identification in the case came in the court's meticulous analysis of its own jurisdiction to put Eichmann on trial. Eichmann was charged under a 1950 Israeli statute called the Nazis and Nazi Collaborators (Punishment) Law, which authorized the punishment of Nazi war crimes, of Nazi crimes against humanity and of what the law called 'act[s] constituting a crime against the Jewish People'. Eichmann's counsel, not surprisingly, challenged the jurisdiction of the court on grounds that the crimes had not taken place on Israeli soil or against Israeli citizens, because the state of Israel did not exist until 1948. The court rebutted this argument in the most explicit way.

The court said that the 'crime against the Jewish people' was nothing more, or less, than genocide as defined in the 1948 Convention on Genocide: acts committed with an intent to 'destroy, in whole or in part, a religious, racial, ethnic or national group as such'.[16] That made it clear that Eichmann was accused of acts that amounted to crimes under international law. Therefore, said the court, 'The question is: What is the special connection between the State of Israel and the offences attributed to the Accused, and whether this connection is sufficiently close to form a

foundation for Israel's right of punishment against the accused.'[17]
Israel, it said, is 'the sovereign state of the Jewish people'. Indeed, the court asserted, quoting the state's founding declaration, it was established by reason of the 'natural right of the Jewish People to be, like every other people, self-governing, in its sovereign state'.[18] Therefore, said the court:

> Even as the Jewish people constituted the object against which the crime was directed, so it is now the competent subject to place on trial those who assailed its existence. The fact that this People changed after the Holocaust from object to subject, and from the victim of a racial crime to the wielder of authority to punish the criminals, is a great historic right that cannot be dismissed. The State of Israel, the sovereign state of the Jewish People, performs through its legislation the task of carrying into effect the right of the Jewish People to punish the criminals who killed its sons with intent to put an end to the survival of this people. We are convinced that this power conforms to existing principles of the law of nations.[19]

This is a powerful and persuasive analysis. Apart from its legal strength, it makes quite clear that the identity of the Jewish people, of the State of Israel and of the judges of Adolf Eichmann are inseparable: Eichmann is being prosecuted and judged by the victims of his crimes. Not the individual victims, but the people and the nation against whom the crime of genocide was committed.

Did the court need to make a point that seems to us so obvious? I believe that it did, not only to vindicate its authority to try and punish Eichmann himself, but to establish the unity of the Jews as a people, and also as a state, under international law. Forty years later, the judgment stands, its integrity intact, its authority unquestioned.

To conclude, the Holocaust was integral to the IMT proceedings in 1945–46, but it was not their centerpiece. It was, however, more than the centerpiece of the Eichmann trial; it was that trial's entire reason for being. There is no contradiction between these poles; they simply reflect the perspectives of the prosecutors and the judges in addressing the issues presented to them. It would be tempting, but inaccurate, to criticize the prosecutors and judges of the IMT for not placing the Holocaust at the center of the trial, and for not devoting more time and more analysis to what we now recognize as the greatest international crime of our own or any era. But we know that the Holocaust did not take place as an isolated process; it was made possible by the campaign of conquest and subjugation that the IMT rightly characterized as a conspiracy and a crime against peace. The trials simply had different purposes, and both still have much to teach us today.

NOTE

1. Raul Hilberg, *Destruction of the European Jews* (New York: Harper Colophn, 1979), first published 1961.
2. http://www.yale.edu/lawweb/avalon/wwii/moscow.htm
3. http://www.yalc.cdu/lawwcb/avalon/imt/jack01.htm
4. Ibid.
5. Raul Hilberg, *Destruction of the European Jews*, p. 365.
6. Ibid., p. 381.
7. Allan A. Ryan, Jr., *Quiet Neighbors: Prosecuting Nazi War Criminals in America*, chapter 1 (New York: Harcourt Brace Jovanovich, 1984).
7. David Wyman, *The Abandonment of the Jews: America and the Holocaust 1941–1945* (New York: Pantheon Books, 1985).
9. http://www.yale.edu/lawweb/avalon/imt/proc/count.htm
10. Drexel Sprecher, *Inside the Nuremberg Trial*, pp. 378–92 (Lanham, MD: University Press of America, 1999).
11. http://www.yale.edu/lawweb/avalon/imt/proc/judwarcr.htm#persecution
12. http://www.yale.edu/lawweb/avalon/imt/jackson/jack63.htm
13. Gideon Hausner, *Justice in Jerusalem* (Jerusalem: Herzl Press, 4th ed, 1977), pp. 288–9.
14. Ibid., pp.291–2.
15. www.ess.uwe.ac.uk/genocide/Eichmann_Index.htm (hereafter 'Eichmann Judgment'), paragraph 1. The judgment was originally given on 12 December 1961.
16. Eichmann Judgment, paragraph 25.
17. Eichmann Judgment, paragraph 32.
18. Eichmann Judgment, paragraph 34.
19. Eichmann Judgment, paragraph 38.

10

Dirty Work: A Personal Reflection on the Irving Trial

ROBERT JAN VAN PELT

In a celebrated meditation in his *Les Misérables*, Victor Hugo declared that the history of men is reflected in the history of the sewers:

> The drain of Paris is an old and fearful thing. It has been a sepulchre, and it has been an asylum. Crime, intellect, social protest, liberty of conscience, thought, theft, all that human laws pursue or have pursued, have hidden in this hole ... The drain is the conscience of the city. Everything converges and is confronted there. In this livid spot there are shadows, but there are no secrets. Everything has its true form, or at least its final form. The pile of ordure has this in its favour, that it tells no lies. Simplicity has taken refuge there ... A sewer is a cynic. It tells everything.[1]

I read Hugo's reflection when I was seventeen, just at the time I decided to become a historian. From my first days as an undergraduate, I realized well that as a historian I would have to descend into a shadowy world, and that most of the historical evidence that comes to us carries the signature of squalor. As a historian, I knew that I would be prepared to make my hands dirty. At times, my hands became quite literally dirty. Joining in my first year an archeological dig in a medieval abbey, I honoured Hugo's observation that 'from the cesspool [the historian] reconstructs the town; from the mud [the historian] reconstructs manners' ,[2] and spent a summer excavating the dried muck of an ancient sump. But even work in the archives proved at times filthy. Dirty bundles of documents, unopened for a century or so, proved quite capable to contain not only the evidence I sought, but also large amounts of grime and dust.

When, much later, I began to study the history of Auschwitz, which the Germans called the Asshole of the World, I often reflected that in the same way that the sewers of Paris had been the conscience and ultimate archive of France, the ruined landscape of Auschwitz was the place where all the history of the West converged in what Hugo called 'a trench of truth', a place where 'filth takes off its shirt. There is an absolute nudity, a rout of illusions and mirage; there is nothing but what actually exists, assuming the ill-omened aspect of that which is over and done with'.[3]

The place made me feel filthy. But, metaphors aside, it was also a place where as a historian I was forced to make my hands dirty. Every day, after eight hours work in the archives, I made a long walk through Birkenau, leaving the paved paths to explore the muddy and soggy fields, the rotting barracks and the crumbling ruins of the crematoria. Every day, I returned to my rented room wet and soiled. Working in Auschwitz, I was reminded that the practice of historical research is not for the fastidious. But while researching the past made me look and sometimes even smell like a sewage worker, like the men who maintain the drains I considered the smutch and smear with pride.

I accepted the invitation to join the defense team assembled to represent Penguin Books and Deborah Lipstadt in the libel suit brought against them by David Irving. I was to serve as an expert witness on the history of Auschwitz. This meant that I was to write an expert opinion that was to present and analyze the evidence of Auschwitz as an extermination camp *qua* evidence. This task was straightforward enough, and I was well prepared for it after many years of research in the archives and at the site itself.

I was also to discuss the various arguments of Holocaust deniers attacking the historical record concerning Auschwitz. I did not look forward to it: a decade earlier, I had considered the writings of deniers in some detail when writing a historiographical study on the problem of relativism in architecture. At that time, I saw Holocaust denial as intimately connected to a postmodern relativism in which questions of historical truth and falsehood are wholly defined within the context of language games and the incommensurability of discourses. However, by the time the book was completed, these particular issues had drifted into the background. In the end only a trace remained: in an endnote, I commented that the hours spent reading the writings of Holocaust deniers 'were among the worst I have had in my professional work'. Defining this literature as an insult to the intellect, I observed that their 'evidence' is doctored, and in their attempts to reveal a great 'conspiracy' to blot the reputation of Germany, these 'scholars' either ignore half of the evidence, and that part of the evidence they attempt to discredit they butcher and mutilate beyond recognition'.[4] It was an angry, visceral outburst that betrayed more than mere intellectual irritation. The negationist tracts had got under my skin in a way that the historical material did not: I felt that I was about to fall into a dangerous personal abyss. I felt dirty – not like a sewer worker, but like someone who had been violated, who had been dispossessed of an important part of his/her identity as a post-Holocaust Jew. To engage the arguments of the deniers, I knew that I was to descend once again into that abyss.

Much of the work of refuting the musings of men like Paul Rassinier and Robert Faurisson was a simple, but extremely tedious, exercise of comparing their statements about the sources to the sources themselves. For example, Faurisson attempted to show that what Auschwitz Kommandant Rudolf Höss had said in his post-war confessions about the gassings in Birkenau was improbable, if not impossible. In order to make his case, Faurisson juxtaposed two of Höss's statements:

> The door was opened a half an hour after the gas was thrown in and the ventilation system was turned on. Work was immediately started to remove the corpses.[5]

> They dragged the bodies from the gas chambers, removed the gold teeth, cut off the hair, then dragged the bodies to the pits or to the ovens. On top of that, they had to maintain the fires in the pits, pour off the accumulated fat, and poke holes into the burning mountain of bodies, so that more oxygen could enter. All these jobs they performed with an indifferent coolness, just as if this was an everyday affair. While dragging the bodies, they ate or smoked. Even the gruesome job of burning the bodies dug up after being in mass graves for a long time did not prevent them from eating.[6]

Closely reading this first passage, Faurisson noted the adverb 'immediately'. In other words, work began immediately when the ventilation began, meaning when the room was still highly toxic. This was very dangerous. It was evident, Faurisson argued, that the Sonderkommando could only have entered the space equipped with gas masks.[7] The second statement by Höss seemed, however, to preclude this, as it recorded that members of the Sonderkommando dragged bodies while eating and smoking. This meant that they could not have been wearing gas masks – probably because of their 'indifferent coolness'. In short, there was an inexplicable contradiction between the extreme toxicity of the gas chamber and the behaviour of the Sonderkommandos. Adding to the collection the official instruction manual of Zyklon B, which stipulated that spaces that had been fumigated with the agent should air out for at least 20 hours, Faurisson came to the conclusion that Höss obviously did not know what he was writing about, and that his testimony was worthless.[8]

Yet on examination, it became clear that Faurisson quoted out of context. The second quotation taken from Höss occurred in the middle of a paragraph that deals with the 'strange' behaviour of the Sonderkommandos. It did not discuss the extermination procedure in any logical order. When Höss mentions that the Sonderkommandos ate or smoked while dragging bodies, he did not say 'while dragging bodies from the gas chambers'. In fact, there was a lot of body-dragging in Auschwitz: in crematoria 2 and 3, bodies were dragged within the incineration halls from the elevator doors to the ovens, in crematoria 4 and 5, bodies were dragged not only from the gas chambers to the morgue, but also from the morgue to the incineration room, and in the case of the open-air burning of the buried corpses in the late summer and fall of 1942, bodies were dragged from the opened mass graves to the incineration pits. At no time did the members of the Sonderkommando need a gas mask for this awful job. Likewise, Faurisson misrepresented the Zyklon B instruction manual. The rule for spaces to be aired for 20 hours applies to rooms without any special ventilation system. After 20 hours of natural ventilation, and another hour with closed windows and doors, the room should be available for all activities except sleeping: this would need yet another day. The situation in the gas chambers was different. With its powerful ventilation system, and with the fact that most of the hydrogen cyanide was absorbed by the victims' bodies, the time could be reduced to 20 minutes.

Comparing the evidence adduced by the deniers to the sources was a tedious labour, but it did not pose a particular moral dilemma. After more than 15 years of marking exams, I had learned how to deal with cheating students. But refuting Faurisson forced me to move beyond identifying the way he misconstrued the historical evidence. I also had to engage with his 'science'. It was a small step from comparing Faurisson's statement about what the Zyklon B instruction manual said about the need to ventilate rooms fumigated with hydrogen cyanide with the original document, to engaging with the scientific question of how quickly a lethal concentration of hydrogen cyanide could be reduced to a harmless concentration in a room of a certain size, using a ventilation system of a certain capacity. This step I was forced to make, because deniers did not limit themselves to misquoting sources, but also invoked scientific arguments to 'prove' that Auschwitz had not been an extermination camp because the gas chambers could not have killed the alleged number of people, or the incinerators could not have incinerated the alleged number of corpses. Fred Leuchter, for example, calculated in his notorious engineering report on the gas chambers in Auschwitz that, over the history of the five Auschwitz crematoria, the total number of people gassed could have been no more than 112,456, and that the maximum number of corpses that could have been theoretically incinerated had been 193,576, while in practical terms the number would have been a little less than half, at 85,092.[9] In other words, the 'alleged' killing of a million people in the Auschwitz gas chambers and the incineration of their bodies in the Auschwitz incinerators had been technologically 'impossible'.

In order to refute Leuchter, I had to go over his premises and his calculations, and take out a pocket calculator myself, and engage in what I considered to be the obscene exercise of showing that the killing of a million people in the Auschwitz gas chambers and the incineration of their bodies in the Auschwitz incinerators had been technologically quite 'possible'. And because Holocaust deniers had argued that the Zyklon B deliveries to Auschwitz had not been sufficient to leave enough hydrogen cyanide to kill the alleged number of victims, I had to write what I consider to be the nauseating nadir of my academic career: a 32-page report on Zyklon B use in Auschwitz (mostly for delousing of garments, barracks and train wagons), showing that, for example, in the year 1943 even the most intensive delousing with Zyklon B would have left a surplus of between 1,660 kg and 3,160 kg Zyklon B available for killing people. This resulted in the following concluding paragraphs:

> How many people can be killed by such an amount? Let us only consider the lower figure of 1,660 kg Zyklon B. The figure given by the Health Institution of the Protectorate Bohemia and Moravia in Prague is that one needs 70 mg of Zyklon B to kill one person. This means that one gram can kill 14 people, or 1 kg 14,000 people. If all the 1,660 kg Zyklon B would be used with 100% efficiency, the surplus of 1,660 kg Zyklon B could have killed (1,660 x 14,000 =)

23.2 million people. But, of course, the efficiency was much lower, as first of all people would absorb more than the minimal lethal dose, and because much Zyklon B would not be absorbed by the victims, but remain in the gas chamber to be pumped out after all had died, and so on. Pery Broad testified that the SS used two 1 kg tins to kill 2,000 people, or 1 kg per 1000 people – a ratio of 1kg per 1,000 people that was also used by Gerstein when he assumed that 8,500 kg of Zyklon B sufficed to kill eight million people. This implies that the 1,660 kg Zyklon B could have killed 1.6 million people. Testifying in Hamburg, Dr. Bendel stated that 1 kg tin was good for the murder of 500 people, which would mean that 1,660 kg Zyklon B would have allowed for the murder of 800,000 people.

It is clear that the extra 1,660 kg to 3,160 kg of Zyklon B available in the camp in 1943 would have more than sufficed to kill the number of 250,000 people murdered in Auschwitz in 1943 with Zyklon B. If we follow Broad's estimate, only 250 kg Zyklon B would have been used for genocidal purposes; if we follow Bendel's estimate, 500 kg would have sufficed.

Using the most conservative estimates possible, Auschwitz had a surplus of Zyklon B of between 3 to 6 times necessary to kill the 250,000 people murdered in Auschwitz in 1943.

Making such repulsive calculations, I felt that I had become loathsome myself.

As long as I was writing at home, my agony was my own. But when I left in January 2000 for England to defend my report under cross-examination, I realized that I faced a difficult situation. On the one hand, I felt a great sense of loyalty to those who had been murdered in Auschwitz, or to the survivors of that camp who would follow the trial in the courtroom and through the media. As a scholar on Auschwitz, I owed it to them to show in posture, language and thought a clear rejection of the obscene phantasmagoria of Holocaust denial. On the other hand, I had to be effective as a champion of truth. I knew that Irving would have the initiative, that he would raise the issues he wanted – from how much Zyklon B it takes to kill a person to how much coke to incinerate a corpse, from how long it would take to empty a gas chamber to how long it would take to burn the bodies – and that I had little choice but to accept and engage with whatever challenge he threw in my direction. I contemplated the possibility of doing both, to honor the victims and defeat Irving, but I did not believe that it would be possible to find a balance.

It so happened that one of the books I had taken with me to London was Nicholas Monsarrat's *The Cruel Sea*, the great novel about the Atlantic convoys that had kept a lifeline between North America and Britain. As I was unhappily considering my options in the courtroom, I read the episode in which a 21 ship convoy heading for Malta was attacked by a pack of U-boats. After six days, 14 ships have been sunk. Finally, as the fifteenth ship goes down, the asdic on the corvette *Compass Rose* picks up an echo of a U-boat. As the ship heads for the target, Lieutenant-Commander Ericson RNR, the captain of the corvette, discovers that the place where the U-boat lay was alive with 40 swimming survivors. Dropping the depth charges would kill these men. The instructions, written by some committee of staff officers at Admiralty, stipulated that in such a situation one should attack at all costs:

> But for a few moments longer he tried to gain support and confidence for what he had to do.
> 'What's it look like now, Number One?'
> 'The same, sir – solid echo – exactly the right size – *must* be a U-boat.'
> 'Is it moving?'
> 'Very slowly.'
> 'There are some men in the water, just about there.'
> There was no answer. The range decreased as *Compass Rose* ran in: they were now within six hundred yards of the swimmers and the U-boat, the fatal coincidence that had to be ignored.
> 'What's it look like now?' Ericson repeated.
> 'Just the same – seems to be stationary – —it's the strongest contact we've ever had.'
> 'There are some chaps in the water.'
> 'Well, there's a U-boat just underneath them.'
> 'All right, then,' thought Ericson, with a new unlooked-for access to brutality to help him: 'All right, we'll go for the U-boat ... ' With no more hesitation he gave the order: 'Attacking – stand by!' to the depth-charge positions aft; and having made this sickening choice he swept in to the attack with a deadened mind, intent only on one kind of kill, pretending there was no other.[10]

Imagining Ericson's agonizing predicament, I realized that he had made the right decision. The heartwrenching choice he had faced helped me to resolve my own dilemma. Having agreed to serve as an expert witness, I would serve the memory of the victims and the dignity of survivors best by making offensive calculations when necessary, drawing distressing diagrams when possible, and taking the court on an abhorrent forensic site visit to the crematoria within the virtual reality created by today's computer programs. This is exactly what I did. It was troublesome, not only to me, but also to those in the courtroom. Witnessing Irving's challenge that the elevator connecting the gas chamber to the incineration room of crematorium 2 was a 'bottleneck' in the whole operation, James Dalrymple described to the readership of the *Independent* what followed:

> Irving knows the value of a strong phrase and the silence in Court 73 seemed to deepen as he said it. We all knew what was coming. Even the judge murmured that he could see where this was leading. How could 500,000 bodies – the number estimated to have died in that one crematorium – be transported up a single lift-shaft, only about 9ft square. Irving demanded that Van Pelt now do the arithmetic of nightmares. How much could the lift carry? 750 kilos, 1,500 kilos, 3,000 kilos? How many bodies would that be at, say 60 kilos a body? Were they in gurneys or were they just squeezed in, like people squashed into a telephone box? How long to take each batch up to the ovens? Ten minutes, or more, each batch? Twenty corpses at a time, or 25?[11]

Dalrymple noted that I entered into the exercise 'reluctantly'. In fact, I was deeply disgusted by Irving's question to make some 'back-of-the-envelope' calculations, and actually did remember Ericson's resolve when I finally answered Irving. My answer was, however, not too clear. Dalrymple, in any case, was not very convinced, and returning that night home in the train he took out his pocket calculator. 'Ten minutes for each batch of 25, I tapped in. That makes 150 an hour. Which gives 3,600 for each 24-hour period. Which gives 1,314,000 in a year. So that's fine. It could be done. Thank God, the numbers add up.' At that moment, Dalrymple was overcome by the obscenity of his calculations. 'When I realised what I was doing, I almost threw the little machine across the compartment in rage.' To him, this minor episode was a normal event in 'the strange and flourishing landscape that has come to be known as historical revisionism':

> It is an area of study with only one subject. The Holocaust. And it is a place where tiny flaws can be found – and magnified – in large structures, where great truths can be tainted and wounded by small

discrepancies, where millions of dead people can be turned into a chimera. And where doubt can be planted like seed in the wind, to grow and fester as the screams of history grow fainter with the years ... A dark and dangerous place where even reasonable people start to do furtive sums on pocket calculators[12]

Indeed. Engaging with Irving's arguments was a messy business, and none of us who stood in the witness box and tried to represent the historical record with honesty, dignity and decency emerged from it with clean hands.

Yet, in the end, from the descent into the sewers of Holocaust history emerged some moment of truth. On April 11, Justice Gray pronounced his judgment. He told the packed court that at the beginning of the trial he had supposed that the evidence of mass extermination of Jews in the gas chambers at Auschwitz was compelling, but that he had 'set aside this preconception when assessing the evidence adduced by the parties in these proceedings.' After going through all the arguments produced by Irving to prove that the 'Factory of Death' could not have worked, and my counterarguments that it had worked sufficiently well to murder all those the Germans intended to kill, Justice Gray stated that:

> having considered the various arguments advanced by Irving to assail the effect of the convergent evidence relied on by the Defendants, it is my conclusion that no objective, fair-minded historian would have serious cause to doubt that there were gas chambers at Auschwitz and that they were operated on a substantial scale to kill hundreds of thousands of Jews.[13]

Hearing these words, I looked up to the gallery, and saw many of the survivors who had attended the trial, and who had looked in horror when Irving raised the issue of the elevator. One of them caught my glance – and winked.

NOTE

1. Victor Hugo, *Les Miserables*, 5 vols (Boston, Estes and Lauriat, n.d.), Vol. 5, p. 129.
2. Ibid., p. 132.
3. Ibid., p. 130.
4. Robert Jan van Pelt and Carroll William Westfall, *Architectural Principles in the Age of Historicism* (New Haven, CT: Yale University Press, 1991), p. 405.
5. Rudolf Höss, *Death Dealer: The Memoirs of the SS Kommanant at Auschwitz*, ed. Steven Paskuly, trans. Andrew Pollinger (New York: Prometheus, 1992), p. 44.
6. Ibid., p. 160.
7. Robert Faurisson, *Mémoire en défense contre ceux qui m'accusent de falsifier l'histoire/La question des chambres à gaz*, preface by Noam Chomsky (Paris: La Veille Taupe, 1980), p. 161.
8. Ibid., pp. 160, 164.
9. Fred A. Leuchter, *The Leuchter Report: The End of a Myth* (Decatur, AL: David Clark, n.d.),

p. 14.
10. Nicholas Monsarrat, *The Cruel Sea* (New York: Knopf, 1951), p. 234f.
11. James Dalrymple, 'The curse of revisionism', *Independent*, 29 January 2000.
12. In the High Court of Justice, London, Queen's Bench Division, *Irving* v. *Penguin and Lipstadt*, daily transcripts, day 33 (Tuesday April 11 2000), p. 33.
13. Ibid., p. 43.

Editors and Contributors

Stephen Eric Bronner is a Professor of Political Science and Comparative Literature at Rutgers University. He is the author of numerous books and articles on European culture and politics. His best-known works include: *A Rumor about the Jews: Reflections on Antisemitism and the 'Protocols of the Learned Elders of Zion'* (St. Martin's Press, 2000); *Ideas in Action: Political Tradition in the Twentieth Century* (Rowman and Littlefield, 1999) and, most recently, *Imagining the Possible: Radical Politics for Conservative Times* (Routledge, 2002).

Tim Cole is a senior lecturer in the Contemporary European Social History Department of Historical Studies at the University of Bristol, UK. He is the author of *Selling the Holocaust* (Routledge, 1999) and is currently completing a study of the spatiality of the implementation and subsequent remembrance of the Holocaust in Budapest, Hungary.

Henry L. Feingold a Professor of History and Director of the Jewish Resource Center at Baruch college and the Graduate Center, City University of New York, and is one of America's most distinguished scholars on the American Holocaust witness role and the reaction of American Jewry to the Holocaust. In this area, his most important books are *The Politics of Rescue: The Roosevelt Administration and the Holocaust, 1938–1945* (Rutgers University Press, 1971) and *Bearing Witness: How America and Its Jews Responded to the Holocaust* (Syracuse University Press, 1995).

Gerald Herman is the Director of Interdisciplinary Studies and an Assistant Professor of History and Education at Northeastern University. His areas of expertise include modern and contemporary European cultural and intellectual history focused on the interrelationships between the arts and the sciences, twentieth-century military history, and history through media. Some of his recent books include *Critical Thinking Skills Using Primary Sources in U. S. History* (Weston Walch Publishers, 2000) and *The Pivotal Conflict: A Comprehensive Chronology of the First World War* (Greenwood Publishing Group, 1992).

Robert L. Hilliard is a Professor of Media Arts at Emerson College, Boston. Among his thirty books are: *Surviving the Americans: The Continued Struggle of the Jews After Liberation* (1997) and *Waves of Rancor: Tuning in the Radical Right*; co-author Michael C. Keith (M.E. Sharpe, 1999). Hilliard is a former Chief of Public Broadcasting at the Federal Communications Commission and former Chair of the Federal Interagency Media Committee.

Debra R. Kaufman is a Professor of Sociology and a Matthews Distinguished University Professor at Northeastern University. She is the author of numerous articles and chapters on women and the professions, feminism, and, more recently, post-Holocaust Jewish identity. Among her best-known books are: *Achievement and Women*, co-author Barbara Richardson (The Free Press, 1982) and *Rachel's Daughters* (Rutgers University Press, 1991). She is the guest editor of *Women and the Holocaust* (Contemporary Jewry, 1996, Vol. 17).

Frederick M. Lawrence is Dean and Robart Kramer Research Professor of Law at George Washington University Law School. A key focus of his career has been federal civil rights enforcement and civil rights crimes. His book on the subject of bias crimes, *Punishing Hate: Bias Crimes Under American Law* was published by Harvard University Press in 1999.

Laurel Leff is an Associate Professor of Journalism at Northeastern University. Her book *Buried by The Times: The Holocaust and America's Most Important Newspaper* was published by Cambridge University Press in March 2005. She was formerly a reporter for the *Wall Street Journal* and the *Miami Herald* and an editor with American Lawyer Media Inc. and the *Hartford Courant*. Leff has a masters in the study of law from Yale University and a masters in communications from the University of Miami.

Martha Minow is the Jeremiah Smith, Jr. Professor of Law at Harvard Law School. Her books include *Between Vengeance and Forgiveness:*

Facing History After Genocide and Mass Violence (Beacon Press, 1998), *Not Only for Myself: Identity, Politics and Law* (The New Press, 1997) and *Making All the Difference: Inclusion, Exclusion, and American Law* (Cornell University Press, 1990). She co-edited *Law Stories* with Gary Bellow (University of Michigan Press, 1996) and has also co-edited casebooks on civil procedure, women and the law, and family law.

David Phillips is a Professor of Law at Northeastern University. He has written extensively in the areas of business ethics, foreign trade and investment, commercial law, corporations, the Uniform Commercial Code and about the role of legal scholarship and law schools in developing nations.

James Ross is the Director of Jewish Studies at Northeastern University. Professor Ross has published three books, *Escape to Shanghai: A Jewish Community in China* (Free Press, 1994), *Caught in a Tornado: A Chinese-American Woman Survives the Cultural Revolution* (Northeastern University Press, 1994) and *Fragile Branches* (Riverhead Books, 2000).

Allan A. Ryan, Jr., formerly Director, Office of Special Investigations, US Dept of Justice, 1980–83, is adjunct Professor of Law Boston College Law School. In addition to teaching human rights law at Boston College Law School, he has participated in several international conferences on how governments should face the crimes of predecessor regimes. Ryan served as a law clerk to Justice Byron R. White of the US Supreme Court from 1970 to 1971, and, in 1983 he conducted the investigation into Klaus Barbie's ties to US intelligence.

Robert Jan van Pelt is a Professor of Architecture at the University of Waterloo in Canada. His most recent book is *The Case for Auschwitz: Evidence from the Irving Trial* (Indiana University Press, 2002). An internationally recognized authority on the history of Auschwitz, van Pelt appeared in Errol Morris's film *Mr. Death: The Rise and Fall of Fred A. Leuchter Jr.* van Pelt chaired the team that developed a master plan for the preservation of Auschwitz, and served as an expert witness for the defense in the notorious libel case *Irving* vs. *Penguin* and *Lipstadt*.

Index

A

Adenauer, Konrad 75
Aebersold, Walter 17
aggressive war (Nuremberg charge) 10, 82–8, 92–3, 102, 104
Allied countries (WW2) air war against German cities 70–1
    Holocaust, knowledge of 67–77, 103
    information strategy 67–77, 94
    see also Soviet Union; United Kingdom; United States of America
American Dissident Voices (neo-Nazi radio programme) 30
American Jewish Committee, the 38, 39
Anschluss, Austrian 84, 95
Anti-Defamation League (ADL) 37–8, 43, 44
anti-Semitism 2, 3, 6, 17, 20–1, 76, 107
Arab states 22, 76
    and hate groups 29–35
    Henry Ford and 9, 25, 27, 28, 30–1, 49
    and modernity 16, 20–1, 22, 23
    Nation of Islam and 37–8
    psychology of 22–3
    uniqueness of 16–17
    see also Holocaust denial; Holocaust, the
Arab states 3, 22, 76
    Protocols of the Learned Elders of Zion and 11, 16, 21, 28, 48
Aryan Nation, the 29
Auschwitz-Birkenau extermination camp 1, 7, 72, 77, 90, 96, 112
    Holocaust denial and 1, 7, 12, 112, 113–16, 118–19
    trials of commandant and guards 10, 91–2
    van Pelt's examination of 3, 8, 112
Austria 84, 95, 96

B

Baumgarten, Arthur 19
Beek, Gottfried zur 17
Beletskii, S.P. 49–50
Belgium 84, 96
Bellis, Mendel, trial of (1913) 26, 33, 49–50
Ben-Gurion, David 61, 77, 107
Bendel, Dr Charles Sigismund 92, 116
Bergen-Belsen concentration camp 10, 91–2, 96
Bernstein, Hermann 49
Between Vengeance and Forgiveness: Facing History After Genocide and Mass Violence (Martha Minow, 1998) 4
Biaha, Dr Franz 89–90
Biarritz (Hermann Goedsche, 1868) 16
Bimko, Ada 92
Birkenau camp *see* Auschwitz-Birkenau extermination camp
Black, Don 33
Black Sox baseball scandal (1919) 16
B'nai B'rith (Jewish organization) 18
Boix, François 90
Broad, Pery 116
Bronner, Stephen 4, 26, 29, 38, 42, 51–2
Brunschvig, Georges 19
Buber, Martin 44
Buchenwald concentration camp 95, 96
Buried by the Times: The Holocaust and America's Most Important Newspaper (Laurel Leff, 2005) 4
Burtsev, Vladimir 49–50
Byrd, James, murder of 29

C

Case for Auschwitz: Evidence from the Irving Trial, The (Professor Robert Jan van Pelt, 2002) 2, 9
Chayla, Armand du 19
Churchill, Winston 27, 69, 71
Clinton, President Bill 32, 39
Cohn, Norman 27
Cold War, the 75, 80
Columbine High School massacre 29
concentration camps 10, 71, 80, 84, 88, 90, 91–2, 95–6, 103
Confederates of the Oath (Swiss newspaper) 17
Congressional investigations, US 38–9
Conot, Robert 89

conspiracy (Nuremberg charge) 57, 83, 110
Convention on Genocide (1948) 108
Coughlin, Father Charles 16
crimes against humanity (Nuremberg charge) 6, 13, 75, 84, 85, 86, 87–8, 105
　general/broad nature of 10, 57, 74
　press reporting of 10, 87–8, 93
　restricted reach of 83
Czechoslovakia 70, 84, 88, 89, 94, 96, 104

D
Dachau concentration camp 89–90, 95–6
Dalrymple, James 118
Daniell, Raymond 82, 86, 93, 95
Dearborn Independent, the 9, 27, 38, 39, 42–3, 49
　Aaron Sapiro lawsuit 28, 40–1
death camps *see* extermination camps
Denying the Holocaust: The Growing Assault on Truth and Memory (Professor Deborah Lipstadt, 1989) vii, 1
Destruction of the European Jews, The (Raul Hilberg, 1961) 7
Dialogue in Hell: Conversations Between Montesquieu and Machiavelli about Power and Justice, A (Maurice Joly, 1864) 16
Displaced Persons Act 104
Displaced Persons, Jewish 74
documentary evidence of the Holocaust 7, 56, 60, 61, 64, 67–8, 81, 96, 107
　Irving v. Penguin UK and Lipstadt viii, 8, 56, 113–16
　of Nazi Germany 6, 7, 58–60, 61, 81, 84–5, 96, 107
Donovan, William 58
Douglas, Lawrence P.
　Eichmann trial 7, 60–1, 63–4
　Nuremberg trials 60–1, 80–1, 83, 84–5, 90, 95–6
Dresden, bombing of viii
Dreyfus affair, the 12, 15, 48–9
Duke, David 31

E
Eden, Anthony 68, 69
Edison, Thomas 25
Egypt 16, 48
Ehrenpreis, Dr Markus 19
Eichmann, Adolf 7, 75, 89
　see also Eichmann trial
Eichmann trial 3, 5, 60–5, 67, 74, 76, 77, 92
　comparisons with Nuremberg 57–8, 60–1, 75, 107, 108
　Jewish identification 102, 107, 108
　legality of 75, 108–9
　press reporting of 4, 10
　prosecution methodology 57–8, 60–3, 64
　television coverage 63
　as 'trial of the Holocaust' 108, 109

witness testimony 7, 57, 60–5
Einsatzgruppen operations 93, 103
empiricism 2, 59
Enlightenment, the 16, 21, 22
Essen, Leon van der 90
Evans, Richard J. viii–ix, 8–9
Evian Conference (1938) 72
Exodus (ship) 74
extermination camps 69, 72, 77, 89–90, 93, 95, 96, 103
　Allied knowledge of 68, 70, 71, 72
　film footage of liberation 80, 105
　see also Auschwitz-Birkenau extermination camp

F
fascism
　American *see* Nazism, American
　European 18, 19–20, 21, 49
　see also Nazism, German
Faurisson, Robert 113–15
Feingold, Henry L. 81
film footage of the Holocaust 80, 84, 89, 95–6, 105
'final solution, the' *see* extermination camps; Holocaust, the
First World War 71
Fischer, Theodor 17, 49
Fleischhauer, Ulrich 17–18
Ford, Henry
　and Adolf Hitler 27–8
　anti-Semitism 9, 25, 27, 28, 30–1, 49
　Bernstein libel case 49
　Jewish campaign against 43
　Protocols of the Learned Elders of Zion and 9, 25, 27–8, 31, 38, 39, 42–3, 49
France 28, 83, 84, 87–8, 96, 106
　Dreyfus affair 12, 15, 48–9
Franco, General Francisco 16
Frank, Anne 63
Frank, Hans 87, 88
free speech and expression 41–2
Freemasons, the 15, 16, 18
Fritsch, Theodor 17
Furrow, Buford 29
Fyfe, Sir David Maxwell 6, 59

G
Gandhi, Mahatma 44
gas chambers 1, 7, 12, 72, 89, 92, 113–15, 119
Geneva Convention, the 70, 71, 83
genocide 3, 13, 27, 52, 105, 106, 108
　Convention on (1948) 108
　current international law 77–8
　see also Holocaust, the
Germany 82
　see also Holocaust, the; Nazism, German
Gestapo, the 88, 89, 107

INDEX

Goedsche, Hermann 16, 18, 48
Goering, Reich Marshal Hermann 85, 93, 105
Gouri, Haim 63
governments in exile (WW2) 68, 69, 70, 72
Gräbe, Hermann 89
Grafton, Samuel 68
Gray, Justice 119
Great in the Small: The Coming of the Antichrist and the Rule of Satan on Earth, The (Sergei Nilus, 1905) 15
Greece 89, 94
Greenspan, H. 63
Guardian, the 2, 3
Guttenplan, D.D. 1, 4–5, 56, 58, 64, 65
Gypsies 88, 105

H

Hague Convention, the 83
Haller, Georg Bernhard 17
Hammer Verlag (publisher, Leipzig) 18
Harrison report (1947) 74
hate crimes 5
hate groups 29–35
Hausner, Gideon 56–7, 60, 61–2, 63, 64, 107–8
Herzl, Theodor 15, 32
Hess, Rudolf 93
Hilberg, Raul 7, 60, 103, 104
Himmler, Heinrich 88, 92
historians vii, viii–ix, 1, 6, 8, 47, 48, 56
 methodology 8–9
history vii–ix, 1, 2, 3, 5, 6–9
 witness testimony 3, 8, 56–7, 58, 59
 see also documentary evidence; truths, historical
Hitler, Adolf viii, 19, 29, 49, 58, 71, 77, 92, 103
 and Henry Ford 27–8
 see also Nazism, German
Hoffman II, Michael A. 2
Holland 104
Holocaust denial vii–ix, 1–8, 11, 76–7
 Allied information strategy (WW2) 67–77, 94
 and Auschwitz 1, 7, 12, 112, 113–16, 118–19
 David Irving and vii–ix, 1, 2, 8, 74, 76, 77, 116, 118, 119
 denier organizations 7, 12
 literature of viii–ix, 112–13
 and press reporting 4, 10–11, 81, 82, 85–91, 96
 prosecution methodology at Nuremberg 83–6, 96
 scientific arguments 114–16
 see also Irving v. Penguin UK and Lipstadt
Holocaust (NBC miniseries) 8
Holocaust, the 2, 5, 7, 13, 91, 102–3, 104–6
 Allied knowledge of 67–77, 103
 centrality of German Nazism 7, 67–8, 77
 documentary evidence 7, 56, 60, 61, 64, 67–8, 81, 96, 107
 Eichmann trial 108–9
 historiography, current 76–7
 Israeli narrative 61–3
 Jewish resistance 7, 61, 91
 journalism and 10, 94–5
 memorial sites and museums 63, 64
 and Nuremberg charges 6, 10, 57, 67, 74, 80–1, 82–4, 86–8, 102
 press reporting at Nuremberg 4, 81, 82, 85–91, 93–4, 96
 Protocols of the Learned Elders of Zion and 25, 26, 27
 'refugee' euphemism 68
 revisionism 1, 107, 118–19
 Shoah (Claude Lanzmann documentary) 63–4
 Soviet bloc concealment 70
 survivor generation, death of 5, 64–5
 survivor testimony *see* survivor testimony, Holocaust
 US attitude to refugees from 35, 68, 73, 74, 94
 see also extermination camps; Holocaust denial
Höss, Rudolf 113–14
House Un-American Activities Committee 39
Hungary 73, 74, 89

I

Illustrated Sunday Herald (UK newspaper) 27
Independent, the 118
Institute for Historical Review 7, 12
Intergovernmental Committee on Political Refugees (IGCPR) 68
International Jew, the 25, 27, 31, 33, 49
International Military Tribunal (IMT) *see* Nuremberg trials
internet, the 1, 47
Islamic websites 32–3, 48, 50
 right-wing hate websites 3, 9, 29, 30, 31–5
Irish Times, the 2
Irving, David
 historical texts viii–ix, 8–9
 Holocaust denial vii–ix, 1, 2, 8, 74, 76, 77, 116, 118, 119
Irving v. Penguin UK and Lipstadt vii–ix, 1, 2, 5, 12, 13, 34, 77, 78
 defence strategy 8–9, 56, 64, 112
 documentary evidence viii, 8, 56
 Eichmann memoir 7, 75
 journalism and 10–11
 judgement viii, 119
 Van Pelt as witness 8, 116–17, 118–19

Islamic websites 32–3, 48, 50
Israel, State of 29, 72, 74, 76, 107, 108–9
  Holocaust narrative 61–3
  Nazi Collaborator Punishment Law (1950) 75, 108
  Palestinian conflict 20, 21, 22, 28, 32
  see also Eichmann trial

J

Jackson, Associate Justice Robert 4, 12–13, 58, 87, 102–7
Jerusalem *see* Eichmann trial
Jewish Supremacism: My Awakening on the Jewish Question (David Duke) 31
Jews, the 12, 44, 94
  Protocols of the Learned Elders of Zion and 3, 15–21, 22–3, 48–50
  Russian pogroms 26
  see also anti-Semitism; Holocaust, the; Israel, State of
Joly, Maurice 16, 18, 31, 48
journalism 9–10, 47, 48, 92–5
  see also newspapers

K

Kaltenbrunner, Ernst 88, 89, 105
Kasztner trial 61
Keitel, Wilhelm 93
Keith, Michael 29
Kempner, Robert 58
Kramer, Josef 10, 91–2
Kristallnacht (9 and 10 November 1938) 73
Ku Klux Klan, the 21, 33

L

LaCapra, Dominic 5
Lampe, Maurice 90
Landsberg concentration camp 88
Lanzmann, Claude 63–4
legal actions vii, 7, 10–11, 23, 26, 28, 50–1
  group libel suits 40, 41–2
  individual libel suits 40–1, 43, 49
  Swiss litigation on the *Protocols* 12, 17–20, 26, 49, 49–50, 51, 52
  see also Irving v. Penguin UK and Lipstadt; legal system
legal system 1, 3, 4, 5, 7, 11–13
  burden of proof 11–12, 50
  'political' trials 12–13, 18, 19–20, 51–2
  Protocols of the Learned Elders of Zion 12, 17–20, 26, 47, 49–51
  'truth claims' and 1, 11, 12, 38–42
  see also legal actions
Legion for Survival of Freedom 7
Leipzig trials (May 1921) 71
Leuchter, Fred 115
Lidice massacre (Czechoslovakia, June 1942) 70, 104

Lie and a Libel, A (Binjamin Segel, trans: Richard Levy, 1995) 28–9
Lindbergh baby kidnapping 26, 40
Lipstadt, Professor Deborah *see* Irving v. Penguin UK and Lipstadt
Lodz ghetto (Poland) 92
Long, Tania 82
Loosli, Carl 19
Lying about Hitler: History, Holocaust, and the David Irving Trial (Richard J. Evans, 2001) 8–9

M

Majdanek extermination camp 95, 96
Marrus, Michael 81, 87, 89, 96
Marshall, Louis 39
Mauthausen concentration camp 90
McCarthy, Senator Joseph 39
McLaughlin, Kathleen 87
McVeigh, Timothy 29, 30, 34
media, the 1, 2, 3, 4, 5, 9–11, 47, 51
  ownership 26–7
  radio 30, 32–3, 48, 50, 52
  right-wing extremism 33
  television 63
  United Kingdom 27
  see also newspapers
Mein Kampf (Adolf Hitler) 49
membership in a criminal organization (Nuremberg charge) 6, 75
Memory of Judgement: Making Law and History in the Trials of the Holocaust, The (Lawrence P. Douglas, 2001) 80–1
Mermelstein, Mel 7, 10, 12
Methon, Francois de 87–8
Meyer, Walter 19
Middleton, Drew 93
Miliukov, Paul 19
Milosevic, Slobodan 78
modernity and anti-Semitism 16, 20–1, 22, 23
Mohammad, Khalid Abdul 37–8, 43
Moscow Declaration on war crimes (1943) 69, 103
Mühlendorf concentration camp 88
Munich peace talks (1938) 84
Murphy, Robert 68

N

Nation of Islam, the 21, 37–8
Nation, The 81
National Alliance, the (USA, neo-Nazi organization) 30, 31
Nazi and Nazi Collaborators (Punishment) Law (Israel, 1950) 75, 108
Nazi Concentration Camp film 84, 95–6
Nazism, American 27–8, 29, 30
Nazism, German 6, 7, 28, 44, 103–4, 106
  centrality of Jewish genocide 7, 67–8, 77

INDEX

documents 6, 7, 58–60, 61, 81, 84–5, 96, 107
and the *Protocols of the Learned Elders of Zion* 16, 17–18, 48
see also Holocaust, the; war crimes, Nazi
'New World Order' (right-wing conspiracy theories) 29–30, 32
New York Post, the 68
New York Times, the 4, 27, 30, 37–8, 81–2
Josef Kramer trial coverage 10, 91–2
Nuremberg trials coverage 10, 81, 82, 85–91, 93, 95–6
newspapers
Nuremberg trials, reporting of 4, 10, 81–2, 85–96
ownership 26–7
Protocols of the Learned Elders of Zion and 26, 27, 28, 31
see also New York Times, the
Nicholas II, Czar 31, 48
Nicolayevsky, Boris 19
Nilus, Sergei 15, 19, 48
Nuremberg trials 3, 4, 5, 12–13, 77
American prosecutors 83–4, 93, 96, 102
British prosecutors 59, 83
charges 6, 10, 57, 67, 74, 75, 82–8, 102, 104–5, 106
see also aggressive war; conspiracy; crimes against humanity
comparisons with Eichmann trial 57–8, 60–1, 75, 107, 108
French prosecutors 83, 87–8
and the Holocaust 10, 57–8, 80–94, 102, 105–6, 109–10
Jewish identification 102
legal framework 82–5, 91, 94
Nazi documents 6, 7, 58–60, 61, 81, 84–5, 96, 107
newspapers' reporting of 4, 10, 81–2, 85–96
prosecution methodology 60–1, 83–6, 92, 96, 102, 105
Soviet prosecutors 58, 83, 88
witnesses 6–7, 57, 58, 84–5, 89, 90

O

Office of War Information (OWI, US agency) 77
Ohlendorf, Otto 90
Ohrdruf concentration camp 84, 96
Oklahoma City bombing 29, 30
Original 8-millimeter Film of Atrocities Against the Jews (film of Warsaw ghetto) 89

P

Palestinian conflict 20, 21, 22, 28, 32
'Patriot' movement (USA) 30
Pell, Robert 73–4
Pelt, Professor Robert Jan van 2, 8, 9

Auschwitz, examination of 3, 8, 112
Irving v. Penguin UK and Lipstadt 8, 116–17, 118–19
Penguin UK *see Irving v. Penguin UK and Lipstadt*
photographs 89, 91
Pierce, Dr William 30, 31, 33–4
Poland 69, 84, 87, 88, 90, 91, 92, 94, 104, 105
extermination camps 68
see also Auschwitz-Birkenau extermination camp
Government in exile 70
Warsaw ghetto 61, 89, 91
postmodernism 13, 39, 112
President's Advisory Committee on Political Refugees (PACPR) 68
Primakov, Yevgeny 30
'Protocols, Bolshevism and the Jews, The' (American-Jewish community leaflet) 43
Protocols of the Learned Elders of Zion 13, 16, 22–3
and the Arab world 11, 16, 21, 28, 48
contents of 17, 29, 48
deconstruction of 6
German versions 18, 26
and hate groups 29–35
Henry Ford and 9, 25, 27–8, 31, 38, 39, 42–3, 49
and the Holocaust 25, 26, 27
Islamic websites and 32–3, 48, 50
the Jew as *chameleon* 17
legal challenges 5, 12, 17–20, 26, 49–51, 52
media coverage 9, 26, 27, 28
methods of challenging 51–2
modern impact and legacy 28–9
origins of 15, 16, 18, 31–2, 48
persistance of falsehood 1, 2–3, 4, 6, 20, 47–52
responses to 38–43
ritual murder (blood libel) allegations 26, 33, 40–1, 49–50
Russian versions (1903, 1905) 15, 26, 48
United States of America and 15–16, 27, 28–35, 38–43, 48, 49
websites, right-wing extremist 3, 9, 29, 30, 31–5
public opinion, 'court of' 5, 6, 42–4, 81
Punishing Hate: Bias Crimes Under American Law (Fred Lawrence, 1999) 4

Q

Quiet Neighbours: Prosecuting Nazi War Criminals in America (Allan Ryan, 1984) 4

R

Rabkin, Jeremy 92, 93
Radio Islam 32–3, 48, 50
Rami, Ahmed 50

Rampton, Richard viii
Rassinier, Paul 113
Ravensbrück concentration camp 90
refugee conference (Bermuda, March 1943) 68
'refugee' euphemism 68
relativism 13, 112
Ribbentrop, Joachim von 93
'Rider without a Horse' (Egyptian television programme) 16
Riegner cable 68
Roll, Ubald von 17–18
Rollin, Henri 48
Roman, Denise 3
Romania 3, 92
Roosevelt, President Franklin Delano 68, 69, 72–4, 94
Rosenberg, Alfred 105
Ross, Alex 95
Rovno (Ukraine) 89
Rublee, George 72–3
Ruby Ridge siege 29
Rumor About the Jews: Reflections on Antisemitism and the 'Protocols of the Learned Elders of Zion', A (Stephen Bronner, 2000) 4, 26
Russia 15, 26, 30, 31, 32, 33, 84, 88, 95, 96
Protocols of the Learned Elders of Zion and 15, 26, 48, 49–50, 50
revolution (1905) 15, 48
see also Soviet Union
Rwandan genocide 52, 78
Ryan, Allan 92, 93

S

Sapiro, Aaron 28, 40–1
Sartre, Jean-Paul 22
Schact, Hjalmar 93
Schnell, Silvio 17, 49
Second World War 3, 4, 28, 57, 59, 84, 93–5
Allied air war against German cities 70–1
Allied information strategy 67–77, 94
governments in exile 68, 69, 70, 72
see also Holocaust, the
Segev, Tom 10–11
Selling the Holocaust (Tim Cole, 1999) 5
Shawcross, Sir Hartley 59
Shepard, Matthew, murder of 29
Shoa Foundation Project 64
Shoa, the *see* Holocaust, the
Shoah (Claude Lanzmann documentary) 63–4
Simpson, O.J., trial of 12
slave labour 71, 72, 84, 88
Smith, Benjamin 29
Smith, Gerald L. K. 31
South Africa 16
Southern Poverty Law Center v. the Aryan Nation 29

Soviet Union 72, 75
approach to German war crimes 69–70, 106
prosecutors at Nuremberg 58, 83, 88
see also Allied countries (WW2); Russia
Spanish civil war (1936-9) 16
Spielberg, Steven 64
SS (Schutzstaffel) 68, 91, 102–3, 105, 116
St James Declaration (18 April 1940) 69
Stalin, Joseph 69–70
Storey, Robert G. 58
Streicher, Julius 87, 105
Surviving the Americans: The Continued Struggle of the Jews After Liberation (Professor Robert Hilliard, 1997) 9
survivor testimony, Holocaust 7–8, 57, 60–5, 84–5, 89, 90, 91–2
D.D. Guttenplan and 5, 56, 57, 58, 64, 65
Sweden 50
Switzerland 32
litigation on the *Protocols* 12, 17–20, 26, 49–50, 51, 52
National Front 17–18, 49
Union of National Socialists 17, 49

T

Taft, President William Howard 43
Taylor, Telford 81, 89, 90
Tehran Conference (1943) 70
Theresienstadt concentration camp (Czechoslovakia) 104
Time magazine 31
Todtli, Boris 18
Truman, President Harry S. 74, 103, 106
'truth claims' 1, 3, 4, 8, 23, 64, 65
Congressional investigations and 38–9
'court of public opinion' 42–4
documentary evidence 59–60
group libel suits 41–2
individual libel suits 40–1, 43
and the legal system 1, 11, 12, 38–42
truths, historical vii, 1, 2, 3–4, 5, 8
documentary evidence 56, 59–60
and relativism 13, 112
and witness testimony 3, 7, 56, 64–5
Turner Diaries, The (Dr William Pierce) 30

U

Ukraine, the 88, 89
United Kingdom 21, 27, 44, 67, 68–9, 91
Foreign Office 72, 73, 77
prosecutors at Nuremberg 59
see also Allied countries (WW2)
United Nations, the 29
United Nations War Crimes Commission (UNWCC) 69, 72, 73, 74
United States of America
American Nazism 27–8, 29, 30

civic culture 21
Congress 27, 32, 38–9, 48
'court of public opinion' 42–4
Holocaust escapees and 35, 68, 73, 74, 94
Holocaust survivor testimony 63
need for Germany as an ally (post WW2) 75
Nuremberg prosecutors 83–4, 93, 96, 102
Office of War Information 77
Protocols of the Learned Elders of Zion 15–16, 27, 28–35, 48, 49
right-wing militias 21, 29
Second World War and 3, 67, 93–4
State Department 68, 72, 73, 74, 77
temporary havens (Free Ports) 68, 74
see also Allied countries (WW2)

V

Valliant-Couturier, Marie-Claude 90
Vatican, the 68
Villard, Oswald Garrison 81–2

W

Waco siege 29
Wagner-Rogers Bill (1939) 73
Walsh, William 88
war crimes, Nazi 3, 12–13
  Allied strategy towards 69–70, 72, 73–4
  Nuremberg charge 57, 83, 84, 85, 86, 87–8, 104–5
  Soviet approach to 69–70, 106
War Refugee Board (WRB) 68, 74
Warsaw ghetto 61, 89, 91
Waves of Rancor: Tuning in the Radical Right
(Robert L. Hilliard and Michael Keith, 1999) 29
Weimar Republic, the 21
Weizmann, Chaim 19
Wiesel, Elie 63
Wilson, President Woodrow 43
Wislicency, Dieter 89
witnesses 91–2
  Eichmann trial 7, 57, 60–5
  Irving v. Penguin UK and Lipstadt 56
  Nuremberg trials 6–7, 57, 58, 89, 90
  Shoah (Claude Lanzmann documentary) 63–4
weaknesses of testimony 7–8, 59
  see also survivor testimony, Holocaust
World Trade Center terrorist attacks (11 September 2001) 33, 34
World Zionist Organization 19
Wyman, David 104

Y

Yad Vashem (Holocaust museum and memorial site, Israel) 63
Yalta Conference (February 1945) 70
Young, Professor James 5, 13
Yugoslavia 88

Z

Zionism 15, 19, 61, 76
Zionist Congress, First (1897) 15, 18, 32
Zuckermann, Antek 61
Zuckermann, Tzivia Lubetkin- 61
Zyklon B 114–1

The Lie that wouldn't die
The Protocols of the Elders of Zion

Hadassa Ben-Itto
Preface by **Lord Woolf**, The Lord Chief Justice
Foreword by **Judge Edward R Korman**

Quote from the Hebrew and German Editions

The history of the Protocols has everything: Forgery, passion, lies, deceit, fascinating historical characters, secret agents, court tension, drama. Were the history of the Protocols made up, it would make riveting, sensational paperback writing. Tragically, it is all true. Nevertheless, Ben-Itto writes her book in a way that brings drama behind the Protocols to life; concentrating on what she understands best- courtroom drama, partcularly the landmark trial in Bern ...'

Jerusalem Post

Of all the libels that have served as a means of incitement of hate against Jews, and as intellectual justification of anti-Semitism, the myth of the so-called 'Jewish Conspiracy' to gain domination of the whole world, as embodied in the forged *Protocols of the Elders of Zion,* is probably the most devious and the most dangerous. Previously only analysed in academic, footnoted studies, the history of the *Protocols* is presented here by Judge Hadassa Ben-Itto in an eminently readable, fascinating account, telling the stories of the numerous people involved over the hundred years that the forgery has existed. Above all, this is the story of a judge who follows the *Protocols* into lawyers' chambers and into courtrooms in Switzerland, in South Africa, in Germany, in the United States and in Russia, and presents the reader with a detailed critical analysis of legal proceedings which culminated in fascinating courtroom drama. The truth is revealed again and again, but the lie wouldn't die.

2005   416 pages
978 0 85303 602 9   cloth   £39.95/$69.50
978 0 85303 595 4   paper   £16.99/$27.50

Confronting the Perpetrators
A History of the Claims Conference

Marilyn Henry

This book is a history of the Claims Conference, the vehicle representing Jewish victims of Nazi persecution for material claims against Germany and Austria

At the end of the twentieth century, the world seemed to rediscover Holocaust survivors. Ceremonies commemorating the 50th anniversary of World War II-era events offered occasions for reflection about the war, its heroes and its victims. In the US, broad interest in the Holocaust was sparked by two cultural phenomena: the 1993 opening of the US Holocaust Memorial Museum and the film Schindler's List. The collapse of communism, the opening of archives in eastern Europe and the approach of the millennium – and with it a desire to 'clean the slate' – also sparked a series of confrontations with the past.

Among those confrontations was an extraordinary focus on the material losses and injuries suffered by Nazi victims. Class-action lawsuits filed in American courts against European governments and enterprises, improvised commissions, national historical reviews and international conferences attempted, at century's end, to deal with the material, historical, legal and moral issues stemming from the Holocaust.

These initiatives built on groundwork laid in 1951, when Israel and an ad hoc consortium of voluntary Jewish organizations received an invitation to negotiate with West Germany for 'moral and material amends' for Nazi-era damages. The consortium became the Conference on Jewish Material Claims Against Germany (known as the Claims Conference).

2006   320 pages
978 0 85303 628 9 cloth £49.50/$79.50
978 0 85303 629 6 paper £20.00/$35.00